Michael Hilb
(Ed.)

Governance of Ecosystems

:Haupt

Michael Hilb
(Editor)

Governance of Ecosystems

The Role of Governance in Collaborative Value Creation

Haupt Verlag

1st edition: 2021
ISBN Print: 978-3-258-08231-8
ISBN E-Book: 978-3-258-48231-6

Cover design and typesetting: Die Werkstatt Medien-Produktion GmbH, Göttingen
Cover illustration: Anatolii Stoiko / Shutterstock.com

All Rights reserved.
Copyright © 2021 Haupt, Berne
Any kind of reproduction without permission of the owner of copyright is not allowed.
Printed in Germany

The Deutsche Nationalbibliothek lists this publication in the Deutsche Nationalbibliografie; detailed bibliographic data are available at: http://dnb.dnb.de

www.haupt.ch

Introduction

There are only a few other strategy concepts that seem to preoccupy managers and board members more today than ecosystems. Every strategy discussion begins with envisioning the future ecosystems and defining the role the organization should play in them. As attractive and compelling as the promises often sound, the problems usually start with understanding what ecosystems are and how they differ from traditional industries.

Even when this challenge is resolved, many attempts to develop ecosystems are doomed to failure. According to a study by BCG (Pidun, Reevevs, and Schüssler, 2020), the main reason, i.e., 34 % of all ecosystem failures, is due to wrong governance decisions. Therefore, ecosystem governance is "a major success factor and a big challenge" at the same time (Pidun, Reeves, and Knust 2020, 1).

The importance of governance to ecosystems is also recognized in the emerging ecosystem theory, as expressed by Jacobides, Cennamo, and Gawer (2018, 2269), "To understand such strategic dynamics, we need a clearer sense of how ecosystems are structured and governed. Behavior in an ecosystem, and ultimately, its success, is affected by the rules of engagement and the nature of standards and interfaces."

It is therefore a great honor to have gathered ten scholars and practitioners to share their insights on ecosystem governance. The contributions are organized into five sections.

The first section examines the *foundations of ecosystem governance*. I begin by examining the transition from corporate to ecosystem governance, followed by Kilian Schmück and Nicolas Gilgen highlighting the importance of incentive mechanisms in ecosystem governance.

The second section offers two *business perspectives on ecosystem governance*. My exploration of the multidextrous nature of value-creating ecosystem strategies is followed by Karin Taheny's article on the role of communication in successful ecosystem adoption.

Two *organizational perspectives on ecosystem governance* follow. While I focus on the role of power in understanding and shaping organizations, Nicolas Bürer highlights the importance of collaboration in ecosystems.

The next section examines two different *legal perspectives on ecosystem governance*. Felix Horber and Christina Lusti examine the applicability of corporate law to the challenges of ecosystem governance, followed by Dante Alighieri Disparte's reflections on structuring ecosystems as associations.

The two concluding articles examine two *applications of ecosystem governance*. Stefano Santinelli describes how he managed to transform a traditional publishing house into a successful business ecosystem. Finally, Ulrich Schimpel shares his experiences with a public-private ecosystem based on distributed ledger technology.

We hope you enjoy reading it, and that the perspectives offered in this book will help you avoid the pitfalls that have confronted many boards attempting to succeed in ecosystems.

Prof. Dr. Michael Hilb						Burgdorf, March 31, 2021

Literature

Jacobides, M. G., Cennamo, C., & Gawer, A. (2018). Towards a theory of ecosystems. Strategic Management Journal, 39(8), 2255-2276.

Pidun, U., Reeves, M., & Knust, N. (2020): How do you manage a business ecosystem? BCG Henderson Institute.

Pidun, U., Reeves, M., & Schlüssler, M. (2020): Why do most business ecosystems fail? BCG Henderson Institute.

Table of Contents

Introduction 5

Section A:
Foundations of Ecosystem Governance 9

From Corporate to Ecosystem Governance
Michael Hilb 11

Governing Democratized Platform Ecosystems
Kilian Schmück and Nicolas Gilgen 23

Section B:
Business Perspectives on Ecosystem Governance 31

Multidextrous Strategy – How to Excel in Platform-driven Ecosystems
Michael Hilb 33

How to Successfully Launch a Digital Ecosystem Business – The Role of Communications
Karin Taheny 43

Section C:
Organizational Perspectives on Ecosystem Governance 51

The Power of Power in Shaping Organizations
Michael Hilb 53

Driving Transversal Collaboration in Ecosystems
Nicolas Bürer 64

Section D:
Legal Perspectives on Ecosystem Governance 71

The Group as a Guiding Model for Ecosystem Governance
Felix Horber and Christina Lusti 73

The Association as a Guiding Model for Ecosystem Governance
Dante Alighieri Disparte............................ 80

Section E:
Applications of Ecosystem Governance 87

Leveraging Digital Ecosystems – How to Transform a Traditional Publisher into a Leading Ecosystem Player
Stefano Santinelli 89

The Role of Governance to Grow Ecosystems – Lessons Learned from a Public-private Distributed Ledger Technology Journey
Ulrich Schimpel................................... 98

Section A:
Foundations of Ecosystem Governance

From Corporate to Ecosystem Governance

Michael Hilb

Abstract
Mastering ecosystems is increasingly seen as key to strategic value creation in highly dynamic environments. The role of governance has become a key differentiator between organizations that win or lose from the ecosystem game. This article discusses the importance of governance to the successful creation, development, and growth of ecosystems and presents eight challenges to be addressed along the ecosystem lifecycle. It continues with a taxonomy of ecosystem governance that provides a menu of effective governance mechanisms to address these challenges. The article concludes with advice on how best to manage the transition from a corporate governance to an ecosystem governance focus.

Author
Michael Hilb is founder and CEO of DBP Group and sits on several boards, such as Klingelnberg, Sigvaris Group, or the International Board Foundation. As a Titular Professor at the University of Fribourg, he teaches strategy, entrepreneurship, and corporate governance at universities in Asia and Europe. Michael Hilb graduated from the University of St. Gallen with an MSc and a PhD, was a Visiting Fellow at Harvard University and INSEAD, and completed several executive education programs at leading business schools.

1 The Emergence and Evolution of Ecosystems

Digitalization is not only transforming societies, economies, and businesses but it also has implications for how different players interact and transact to deliver economic value. There are four implications that are often highlighted when describing this new form of value creation:

1. **From asset ownership to asset orchestration:** As digitalization enables more effective ways to allocate resources, the focus of activities has shifted from creating value for tangible assets to orchestrating their use as highlighted by Iansiti and Levien (2004, 25): "Strategy is becoming, to an increasing extent, the art of managing assets that one does not own."
2. **From pipelines to platforms:** As a result, the orchestrators, or platforms as they are often called, are able to capture more value than the manufacturers as highlighted by Gawer and Cusumano (2002) or Parker, Van Alstyne and Choudary (2016) in their description of the "platform economy."
3. **From competition to co-opetition:** As an orchestrator by definition relies on others to produce and consume, the relationship between the different players goes beyond pure competition. Or as Birkinshaw (2020, 11) highlights: "(The platform's) aim is to maximize the number of people coming through the turnstile, rather than increase the height of the fence or the width of the moat."
4. **From industries to ecosystems:** This eventually leads to structural changes in the space where companies operate. While the strategic focus used to be on industries, it increasingly shifts to "ecosystems" (e.g. Ramírez and Mannervik 2016 or Williamson and Meyer 2020).

Welcome to the ecosystem economy. Business ecosystems, which is a term that can be traced back to Moore (1993, 1996), have gained escalating attention over the last decade although the discussion actually dates back more than 30 years (Rietveld and Schilling, 2020).

Based on the initial definition by Moore (1996, 26), who described it as "(a)n economic community supported by a foundation of interacting organizations and individuals – the organisms of the business world," other academics have refined the term over time.

Adner (2017, 40), for instance, highlighted the importance of "the alignment structure of the multilateral set of partners that need to interact in order for a focal value proposition to materialize." The value proposition is at the center of the definition by Ramírez and Mannervik (2016, 46), who stress that we should "(think) of value as co-created – not added – by two or more actors in a relationship, synchronically as well as sequentially." Jacobides, Cennamo, and Gawer (2018, 2264) extend the understanding of ecosystems by stressing that there are "actors with varying degrees of multilateral, non-generic complementarities that are not fully hierarchically controlled." From a governance perspective, this means "that their members all retain residual control and claims over assets" (2266) and "that ecosystems need to be both de jure and de facto run with decision-making processes that are to some extent distributed" (2266).

2 The Role of Governance in Value Creation in Ecosystems

This brings us to ecosystem governance, which is a key aspect of ecosystems as highlighted by Rietveld and Schilling (2020) or Jacobides, Cennamo, and Gawer (2018). How are interests aligned in the first place? How are these interests orchestrated effectively and fairly? Finally, how can governance maintain and develop as the ecosystems evolve?

This is also reflected in business practice: The failure of building or maintaining ecosystems is often attributed to a lack of effective ecosystem governance (Pidun, Reeves, and Schlüssler 2020). As a result, Fenwick, McCahery, and Vermeulen (2019) propose the need for a distinct "platform governance". In line with the arguments above, the notion should be extended to "ecosystem governance".

This paper proposes the "ecosystem-as-governance" view. This builds on two conceptualizations proposed by Adner (2017): the "ecosystem-as-structure" approach, which takes an activity-centric view of interdependence, and the actor-centric "ecosystem-as-affiliation" perspective.

2.1 The Ecosystem-as-affiliation Perspective

An important first step for discussing ecosystem governance is to better understand the different types of actors involved in an ecosystem and the roles that they may play. There is common agreement that different players interact in ecosystems. One player usually takes a lead, which some call "keystone" (Iansiti and Levien 2004) or "orchestrator" (Jacobides, Cennamo, and Gawer 2018). It is in the nature of ecosystems that only few players can be orchestrators (Greeven 2020).

Alongside the orchestrator are other important roles. I suggested in an earlier publication (Hilb 2020a) that five distinct roles can be found in ecosystems:

The Platform Orchestrator, Feeder, User, Aggregator and Enhancer. These five players pursue distinctive interests, provide unique contributions and bring their own expectations to an involvement in ecosystems.

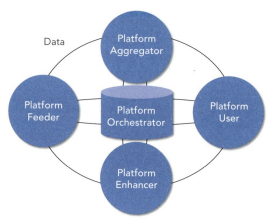

Exhibit 1: Platform Forces | platformforces.com

2.2 The Ecosystem-as-structure Perspective

The second perspective proposed by Adner (2017) places the structure of an ecosystem at the center. Three structural dimensions are usually highlighted as Closed vs. Open, Centralized vs. Decentralized and Interaction vs. Transaction-focused ecosystems.

For Pisano and Verganti (2008), the choice between closed and open ecosystems is defined by the access conditions. They argue that closed ecosystems function well if the number of relevant problem solvers are small and known, whereas open ecosystems are recommended if the evaluation of the user quality is easy and everybody can contribute to the solutions. A similar explanation is offered to elaborate on the rationale for centralized vs. decentralized ecosystems. They suggest a centralized solution if the orchestrator has the capability to assess the solutions while preferring a decentralized approach if no single player can do so.

Finally, many authors stress the difference between interaction and transaction-focused ecosystems. While interaction-based ecosystems focus on the exchange of information and data, transaction-focused ecosystems promote the exchange of goods and services.

2.3 The Ecosystem-as-governance Perspective

While the actor- and activity-centric perspectives are important to understand value creation in ecosystems, one central aspect is not yet addressed: how to direct and control those actors and their activities?

In order to discuss the most suitable governance mechanisms for ecosystems, it is worthwhile looking at the generic governance modes. While most distinguish between market- and hierarchy-based governance (e.g. Jacobides, Cennamo, and Gawer 2018), I propose adding a third fundamental governance mode, community-based governance as suggested by Minnaar (2020).

How do the three governance modes differ?

1. **Market-based governance:** This describes any coordination of economic activity that is based on transactional contracts, such as for trading goods, services, and data. As the terms and conditions of the transactions are clearly defined, so are the consequences if contracts are breached. Hence, all parties have full control but little incentive to develop beyond the contractual obligations.
2. **Hierarchy-based governance:** If organizations hire staff, they believe it is more efficient to internalize the market. In that case, the coordination is based on instructions within the framework defined by labor laws or labor contracts. In order to increase the efficiency of employees, the employers are incentivized to train them.
3. **Community-based governance:** In this case, there is little more than a constitution which lays out the basic rules of the interactions. All parties agree on these rules and believe they can act upon them without needing any further enforcement mechanisms. Hence, this governance mode requires a trust-based relationship.

	Market-based Governance	Hierarchy-based Governance	Democracy-based Governance
Result Focus	Individual	Shared	Mutual
Codification	Transaction Contract	Labor Contract	Constitution
Orchestration	Control	Coordination	Cohesion
Value Driver	Transparency	Training	Trust
Product Value	Commoditized	Customized	Complementary

Exhibit 2: Governance Modes | governancemodes.com

With regard to ecosystems, all three forms of governance are displayed. First of all, most players are in market-based relationships with each other, e.g. the behavior of Platform Users and Feeders versus Orchestrators are usually governed by transaction contracts. As many of the actors are firms, they apply hierarchy-based governance mechanisms within their organizations.

At the same time, some actors also apply community-based governance mechanisms when engaging in relationships that go beyond pure market and hierarchy-based governance mechanisms. For instance, the business relationships between a Platform Orchestrator and an Aggregator or an Enhancer are often characterized by a complementary value proposition as defined in the co-opetition model (Nalebuff and Brandenburger 1996 or Brandenburger and Nalebuff 2021). As stated by Jacobides, Cennamo, and Gawer (2018, 2261): "What sets ecosystems apart from market-based arrangements is that end customers choose from a set of producers or complementors who are bound together through some interdependencies."

3 The Challenges of Ecosystem Governance

As highlighted by both academics (e.g. Rietveld and Schilling 2020 or Jacobides, Cennamo, and Gawer 2018) and practitioners (e.g. Pidun, Reeves, and Schlüssler 2020), ineffective governance of ecosystems is considered one of the main reasons for failure in creating, developing and, in particular, maintaining ecosystems. This was confirmed by Moore (1993), such that the nature of ecosystems, and hence the challenges that come with them, differ by the stage of the ecosystem evolution. In line with Moore's four stages, i.e. birth, expansion, leadership, and self-renewal, we shall apply the FACE lifecycle model (Hilb 2020b) to describe the eight primary challenges in ecosystem governance:

Formation stage
a. **Matching challenge:** The initial challenge of building an ecosystem is to identify parties that can contribute to it and match the different interests. As none of the players usually knows all potential partners, this process is often iterative.
b. **Alpha animal challenge:** Even if all the key parties are identified and assembled, there is often a tendency that many players want to take the lead. As ecosystems only can live with one Orchestrator, the different actors need to find the most suitable role which may not be that of the Orchestrator.

Acceleration stage
a. **Access challenge:** As ecosystems evolve and grow, future expansion will depend on new parties becoming involved. This may lead to a rebalancing of power structures among existing actors if, for example, direct competitors join the ecosystem.
b. **Consensus challenge:** This creates the next challenge, i.e. defining and agreeing on common access rules as the ecosystem grows. As some parties may get stronger from developing the ecosystem, this may reduce the influence of other actors. This can make it difficult to reach consensus.

Consolidation stage
a. **Self-interest challenge:** As ecosystems start consolidating, the interests of each party return to the center stage. While the focus in the growth phase is to grow the pie, sharing the pie becomes central in the consolidation phase. This may lead to a number of challenges for finding agreement among all parties.
b. **Benefit challenge:** At the same time, the question about who benefits becomes a contentious issue as rules need to be defined about how to share the profit in the future. Some players may not agree and join other ecosystems instead.

Exit or Energization stage
a. **Priority challenge:** At some point, the players involved must decide whether the ecosystem has reached its expiry date or whether it is worth being rejuvenated. Here, the priorities among the actors may differ, and not all parties may be willing to remain a part of the game.
b. **Commitment challenge:** At this point, the true commitment of all parties involved is tested. Have they viewed the ecosystem mainly as a project to explore and develop capabilities, or are they committed to staying for the long term? The answer to this question may differ among the parties involved.

In addition to the stage-specific challenges, McGrath (2020) stresses the importance of strategic inflection points in determining the right time to join an ecosystem. This is because the expectations of value creation potential of an ecosystem can differ over time. An underestimation of the value creation potential in the beginning may be followed by a phase of hyped expectations, which will hopefully settle into a more realistic estimation.

4 Approaches to Effective Ecosystem Governance

How can we best apply these governance mechanisms to address the challenges outlined above? Apart from purely market- and hierarchy-based governance modes, there are several other governance modes that should be considered in the context of ecosystems. We shall distinguish four of these modes, i.e. cooperation, collaboration, consortium and confederation, whereof the first two are derived from Himmelmann (2002) and the third from Pisano and Verganti (2008).

1. **Cooperation:** The simplest form of transactional interaction between two or more parties involves clearly defined expectations by all parties.
2. **Collaboration:** This mode refers to a repetitive interaction between multiple parties with clearly defined expectations.
3. **Consortium:** On the other hand, a consortium functions within clearly defined rules and a time frame to achieve a common goal.
4. **Confederation:** A confederation refers to a standard set of rules that regulates basic issues, such as data rights or value creation.

As discussed above, there are two ways any governance mode can be formalized and codified, either by contract or by constitution. While contracts state the details of pre-defined transactions or interactions, a constitution lays out the basic principles and provides guidance for those committing themselves to the respective constitution. If we take the two codifiers as a framework, we can depict the four modes on a continuum.

Exhibit 3: The contract-constitution continuum

How can we decide which mode should be applied to ensure effective governance of ecosystems? The optimal governance mode mix depends on two criteria:

– **Objective:** The first question is about the objective of the ecosystem: Do the different players expect a shared output or outcome? Outputs are defined as tangible results of an interaction, e.g. new products or customers, whereas outcomes define the end-state, e.g. market or innovation leadership.

- **Time horizon:** Secondly, it is vital that the players are aligned in their understanding of the time horizon of an ecosystem: Do they see the interaction as a finite or infinite game? Here, we refer to Carse (2011) who coined the dichotomy. He distinguished between interactions "for the purpose of winning", versus infinite games that are "for the purpose of continuing the play." Ramírez and Mannervik (2016) stress that many ecosystems resemble indefinite games as actors play multiple roles at the same time, e.g. as consumers and producers.

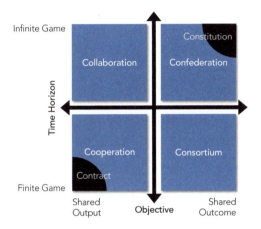

Exhibit 4: Ecosystem Governance | ecosystemgovernance.com

Given the complexities of ecosystems, and the variety of roles different players assume in an ecosystem, the optimal outcome is usually a mix of governance modes applied concurrently. Nevertheless, it is important to define the dominant mode to avoid unnecessary target conflicts.

To reach this consensus is not easy. As the assessment of the two dimensions may vary among players, it is pertinent to ensure alignment. A lack of such alignment is likely to lead to governance failure. Therefore, a clear process should be established to agree on common assumptions. Furthermore, this process needs to be performed repetitively to take into account the different requirements as the ecosystem evolves. What is needed to make this happen? First and foremost, we need to move mentally from corporate to ecosystem governance.

5 Mastering the Transition from Corporate to Ecosystem Governance

The transition from corporate to ecosystem governance is more than just an extension of the scope of corporate governance. It brings a fundamental shift in perspectives and mindsets of those involved, and may also create overlapping dilemmas:

1. **Competitor vs. collaborator:** The strategic imperative changes from a pure competitive to a co-competitive mindset. This may have implications for the decision makers charged with control and direction, as other ecosystem players must be viewed as competitors and partners at the same time.
2. **Today vs. tomorrow:** Ecosystems are designed to create future value. This implies the increasing relevance of a future-oriented mindset with a continued focus on ensuring current performance.
3. **Exploitation vs. exploration:** In line with the above, companies need to refocus from exploitation of the existing status quo towards exploration of new business models. At the same time, the current business needs to continue succeeding.
4. **Company vs. cosmos:** Finally, this leads to an extended focus of governance that reaches beyond the firm's boundary. This will include other parties in the ecosystem, their interests and contributions while preserving the company's own interests.

Mastering these fundamental dilemmas requires boards to embark on four mental journeys:

1. **From value addition to value co-creation:** As suggested by Ramírez and Mannervik (2016), the value creation approach changes fundamentally in ecosystems. The focus is no longer on each party adding value but rather on co-creating it. This principle needs to guide any decisions in ecosystem governance.
2. **From planning to experimenting:** The co-creation focus has a direct impact on the predictability of the value creation outcomes. As detailed planning becomes more challenging, or even impossible, a disciplined approach to experimenting must become the accepted, or even encouraged, method for governance decisions.
3. **From secrecy to transparency:** Given the co-competitive nature of the relationship between the parties of an ecosystem, open communication and access to information becomes critical to ensuring smooth interactions and transactions.

4. **From control to influence:** Finally, governance bodies should acknowledge that activities can no longer be controlled in the way they were within the boundaries of a company. An influencing attitude replaces the established command – and – control approach.

As with any journey, there is usually no direct route. There are several junctions along the way and different decisions have to be taken at each stage. At the same time, there are many discoveries to be made. Tools, such as a map or a compass, can be useful. The concepts presented in this article hopefully serve as practical tools for navigating the mental journey from corporate governance to ecosystem governance.

Literature

Adner, R. (2017). Ecosystem as structure: An actionable construct for strategy. Journal of management, 43(1), 39-58.

Birkinshaw, J. (2020). Turnstile logic: The new rules of strategy in an ecosystem world. In: Ecosystem Inc.: Understanding, harnessing and developing organizational ecosystems. Crainer. S. Thinkers50. London, UK.

Brandenburger, A., & Nalebuff, B. (2021). The rules of co-opetition. Harvard Business Review, 1, 48-57.

Carse, J. (2011). Finite and infinite games. Simon and Schuster, New York, NY.

Fenwick, M., McCahery, J. A., & Vermeulen, E. P. (2019). The end of 'corporate' governance: hello 'platform' governance. European Business Organization Law Review, 20(1), 171-199.

Gawer, A., & Cusumano, M. A. (2002). Platform leadership: How Intel, Microsoft, and Cisco drive industry innovation (Vol. 5, pp. 29-30). Harvard Business School Press, Boston, MA.

Greeven, M. (2020). The end of strategy in business ecosystems? In: Ecosystem Inc.: Understanding, harnessing and developing organizational ecosystems. Crainer. S. Thinkers50, London, UK. 79-86.

Hilb, M. (2020a). Cracking the collaboration codes – How to succeed in ecosystems. In Governance of Ventures, Hilb, M. 97-106. Haupt, Bern, CH.

Hilb, M. (2020b). Venture governance – The hidden value driver of entrepreneurial value creation. In Governance of Ventures, Hilb, M. 11-23. Haupt, Bern, CH.

Himmelmann, A.T. (2002). Collaboration for a change: Definitions, decision-making models, roles, and collaboration process guide. Himmelman Consulting, Minneapolis, MN.

Iansiti, M., & Levien, R. (2004). The keystone advantage: what the new dynamics of business ecosystems mean for strategy, innovation, and sustainability. Harvard Business Press, Boston, MA.

Jacobides, M. G., Cennamo, C., & Gawer, A. (2018). Towards a theory of ecosystems. Strategic Management Journal, 39(8), 2255-2276.

McGrath, R. (2020). Ecosystem maturity and the stepping stone strategy. In: Ecosystem Inc.: Understanding, harnessing and developing organizational ecosystems. Crainer. S. Thinkers50, London, UK. 113-119.

Minnaar, J. (2020). The age of community capitalism. In: Ecosystem Inc.: Understanding, harnessing and developing organizational ecosystems. Crainer. S. Thinkers50, London, UK. 120-132.

Moore, J. F. (1996). The Death of Competition: Leadership & Strategy in the Age of Business Ecosystems. HarperBusiness, New York, NY.

Moore, J. F. (May–June 1993). Predators and prey: A new ecology of competition. Harvard Business Review. pp. 75–86.

Nalebuff, B., & Brandenburger, A. (1996). Co-opetition. HarperCollinsBusiness, London, UK.

Parker, G. G., Van Alstyne, M. W., & Choudary, S. P. (2016). Platform revolution: How networked markets are transforming the economy and how to make them work for you. WW Norton & Company, New York, NY.

Pidun, U., Reeves, M., & Schlüssler, M. (2020). Why do most business ecosystems fail? BCG Henderson Institute.

Pisano, G. P., & Verganti, R. (2008). Which kind of collaboration is right for you. Harvard Business Review, 86(12), 78-86.

Ramírez, R., & Mannervik, U. (2016). Strategy for a networked world. World Scientific Publishing Company, Singapore, SG.

Rietveld, J., & Schilling, M. A. (2020). Platform competition: A systematic and interdisciplinary review of the literature. Journal of Management, 0149206320969791.

Williamson, P. J., & De Meyer, A. (2012). Ecosystem advantage: How to successfully harness the power of partners. California Management Review, 55(1), 24-46.

Williamson, P. J., & De Meyer, A. (2020). Ecosystem Edge: Sustaining Competitiveness in the Face of Disruption. Stanford University Press, Stanford, CA.

Governing Democratized Platform Ecosystems

Kilian Schmück and Nicolas Gilgen

Abstract
Platform ecosystems have been around for a long time. Many of the current highly successful companies such as *Amazon, Google,* and *Facebook* have taken advantage of platforms in their meteoric rise. However, centralized data ownership, lock-in effects, and market power of centralized platform owners are increasingly raising questions about regulating monopolistic market structures. The solution to the problem may lie in democratized platform ecosystems. Initiated by a consortium or foundation, democratized platform ecosystems create the underlying infrastructure for fair competition. However, developing, managing, and expanding a platform that ultimately belongs to no one requires sound governance.

Authors
Kilian Schmück is a research assistant and project manager at the Institute of Technology Management at the University of St. Gallen. His research focus lies on democratized platform ecosystems, ecosystem governance, and corresponding incentive mechanisms. He is the initiator of the St. Gallen Blockchain Roundtable, where scientific research on democratized platforms is discussed together with business, academia, and politics. Kilian received his Master of Science at the RWTH Aachen University in Mechanical Engineering.

Nicolas Gilgen is a research associate at the St. Gallen Institute of Management in Asia, the University of St. Gallen's institute in Singapore. His research focuses on innovation in small and medium-sized enterprises. Previously, Nicolas studied Business Innovation and International Management (CEMS) at the University of St. Gallen and Ivey Business School in Canada.

1 Introduction

Platform ecosystems have been around for centuries. The marketplace in the Middle Ages is nothing more than an analog "platform" ecosystem governed by a local authority. New technologies and products such as the PC, the internet, and smartphones enabled the rise of new dominant platform players. Between 1980 and 2000, for example, *Microsoft* achieved a dominant position by applying a licensing business model and generating and exploiting network effects. *Amazon,* founded in 1994, leveraged the then largely untapped potential of e-commerce to become one of the most valuable companies in the tech industry today. However, recent headlines about tax evasion, poor working conditions, and data security concerns have cast the tech giants in a bad light. As a result, there are growing voices calling for regulation and new means for value capture mechanisms in platform ecosystems, and even the breaking up of tech monopolies altogether. Indeed, there are several challenges associated with centralized platforms. For example, the rise of digital platform players has led to data monopolies, resulting in a lack of grassroots innovation. One can only imagine what innovations would emerge if pioneering startups had access to the vast amounts of data held by the tech giants. Another example is the subjectively unfair market conditions, such as some ridesharing companies' transaction fees of up to 30% in some markets, resulting from information asymmetries between the platform owner and users.

But the solution to these problems does not necessarily lie in breaking up platform companies. Digital platforms do offer significant advantages, such as immense efficiency gains and transaction cost reductions. Instead, the solution should lie in a drastic rethinking of how platforms are initiated and managed in the first place. The result is democratized platform ecosystems. By applying and combining appropriate governance models and novel technologies such as blockchain, democratized platform ecosystems open up a new value space for all participants.

As a first step, this chapter takes a closer look at the first governance model of federated platform ecosystems, which has strong similarities to traditional business ecosystems. It then discusses how the second governance model, the one of decentralized platform ecosystems, creates a neutral, underlying technological infrastructure for applications. Finally, the chapter briefly discusses when to choose one or the other.

2 Federated Platform Ecosystems: Initiating Democratized Platform Ecosystems through Consortia

In a business ecosystem, a diverse group of companies comes together to jointly create a new or superior value proposition that could not be achieved by a single company alone. In this sense, a business ecosystem is an interactive, collaborative configuration of business models from a customer journey perspective. A leading company, the orchestrator, orchestrates the configuration of the different business models within a business ecosystem.

Federated platform ecosystems are very similar: several organizations, usually incumbents, join together to solve a specific, cross-industry problem. This could be, for example, putting ownership and management of identity data back into the hands of data creators or making trade finance more automated, efficient, and transparent. For instance, the *IDUnion* network deploys self-sovereign identity (SSI) technologies and other distributed ledger technologies (DLTs) such as blockchain to create an efficient and secure identity solution for natural persons, legal persons as well as machines. The project is supported by the *German Federal Ministry of Economics,* and the consortium currently includes the *Main Incubator/Commerzbank, Bundesdruckerei, Bosch, the Technical University of Berlin, Deutsche Bahn, BMW, Deutsche Börse, Telekom Innovation Laboratories*, the *City of Cologne,* and *Siemens*. The goal is to create a digital login like Gmail or Facebook login, but with a decentralized structure, so that the identities themselves remain in the owner's sovereignty. Although these ecosystems are often initiated by a single company that later takes on orchestration, the platform created may not be owned by any one party. Centralized platform ownership would run counter to the very idea of these ecosystems: to create open standards for different solutions and achieve network effects without lock-ins. In such an environment, the best solution wins because interoperability allows users to easily "lift and shift" their data to the preferred provider. This is enabled in no small part by DLTs that are data ledgers shared and maintained by a network of users rather than by a central party. Therefore, DLTs rely on consensus mechanisms that define how consensus on the state of the ledger is reached. By eliminating intermediaries, DLTs solve the aforementioned matters of centralized data ownership, lock-in effects, and the resulting market power of dominant platform owners.

However, in federated platform ecosystems, a fundamental challenge arises: how can organizations be incentivized to invest in creating a platform that they do not ultimately own? Sound governance is needed to solve these game-theoretic challenges. Platform governance can be broadly defined as the configuration of decision rights, accountability, and incentive mechanisms. In federated platform ecosystems, decision-making power is centralized among consortium members who work collaboratively to realize a common goal. Therefore, platform governance is not necessarily openly accessible to external third parties. Rather, access is governed by specific criteria designed to ensure complementarity among the governing consortium members. Accountability is established through traditional means. Contracts, legal entities such as associations and cooperatives, and consortium members' reputations create accountability and trust. This is also necessary because, unlike decentralized platform ecosystems, federated platform ecosystems simply reflect consortium governance in the technology, rather than implementing governance "on-chain," i.e., in DLTs. In terms of incentive mechanisms, each consortium member typically has an internal business case that justifies the organization's investment in the project. For example, banks have an incentive to invest in more efficient data management or trade finance solutions to save significant onboarding and paperwork costs. This is not to say that consortia formation is easy. Because corporate decision-making power is often based on profitability and return on investment considerations, investing in a platform that does not provide direct financial benefits can be challenging to justify internally. There often seems to be a disconnect between incentive mechanisms and business models. Business models contain the value creation mechanisms of a focal company. Thus, they relate to a specific value proposition to effectively satisfy customer needs. New business models with new profit potentials can indeed result from federated platform ecosystems – especially if democratic access to data is enabled. However, due to the early stage of DLTs and democratized platform ecosystems, new business models and revenue streams are still elusive in many cases. Incentive mechanisms, in turn, motivate companies to participate in the development and maintenance of federated platform ecosystems in the first place. Attempting to establish a connection between incentive mechanisms and business models in a company can lead to a chicken-and-egg problem.

3 Decentralized Platform Ecosystems: Initiating Democratized Platform Ecosystems through Non-profit Foundations

Decentralized platform ecosystems are typically initiated by non-profit foundations that develop the initial version of the technology platform (or the DLT protocol), which often serves as the technological basis for federated platform ecosystem or decentralized applications (DApps). Examples are the *Ethereum Foundation* initiating *Ethereum*, the *Tezos Foundation* initiating *Tezos*, the *Hyperledger Foundation* curating the *Hyperledger Protocols*, or the *Web3 Foundation* initiating and curating *Polkadot*. Compared to a federated platform, the value proposition for a decentralized platform is much broader; a decentralized platform creates the underlying infrastructure on which virtually any use case can be realized. As mentioned, this may very well include applications for identity data management or trade finance, such as *IDUunion*. To access this value and evolve the decentralized platform ecosystem beyond its early stages, governance must be translated into technology. Therefore, the goal of decentralized platform ecosystems is to initiate the transition from off-chain (*Ethereum, Hyperledger*) to on-chain (*Polkadot, Tezos, Ethereum 2.0*) governance. While the foundation takes a central role in developing the platform initially, it can hand over further development to the network participants with the on-chain implementation of governance. The result is an open-access, truly democratized platform ecosystem. Barriers to entry are kept as low as possible to allow any willing party to participate in the governance of the ecosystem. On-chain governance mechanisms, such as token-based voting on proposals from the community, ensure the ability to adapt the decentralized platform governance model to changing ecosystem and environmental needs. As a result, the democratized platform ecosystem achieves a commercially desirable state. Transaction costs are low due to automation and mature processes. Trust in traditional institutions is replaced by trust or even truth in the technology. As with the federated platform ecosystem, the cooperative dynamic leads to the greatest value creation, as it is not the actor with the most extensive network effects that prevails, but the one with the best resource configuration to solve a given problem with its application.

To raise funding for developing the first version of the technological platform, the foundation issues tokens and sells them to crowd investors. This process is often referred to as an initial coin offering (ICO) or token generation event (TGE). DLTs have thus not only led to new opportunities in the governance of the ecosystem but also democratized early-stage investing, at least to some degree. These tokens are then used as payment and coordination functionality within the platform ecosystem and the platform governance, as well as an incentive mechanism for establishing network effects.

4 Federated or Decentralized Platform Ecosystem: Choosing the Right Governance Model

The development of democratized platform ecosystems has just begun. Examples are still rare, and the space is expected to grow and evolve in the coming years. Arguably, there are initiatives that fall somewhere between the two models discussed. Nevertheless, federated platform ecosystems such as *IDunion* and decentralized platform ecosystems such as *Polkadot* and *Tezos* demonstrate the potential of these new forms of ecosystems and ecosystem governance.

Initial research into democratized platform ecosystems offers first insights:

A key difference between federated and decentralized platform ecosystems lies in the locus of platform governance and democracy. On the one hand, in federated platform ecosystems, governance is anchored in the law and reflected only in the technology ("law is code"). Governance thus resides with the legal entity, which has very democratic governance processes. On the other hand, in decentralized platform ecosystems, governance is cast in code ("code is law"). Therefore, on-chain governance enables a truly decentralized and democratic governance process that builds trust on its own and does not rely on legal institutions.

Federated platform ecosystems are suitable for addressing defined use cases and solving specific problems. In particular, where consortium formation is possible due to company-inherent incentives, it may make sense to opt for a federated platform ecosystem. One advantage then is that the consortium can still retain significant decision-making power over platform development by forming an association or cooperative. This can be advantageous if consortia want to create a counterpart to dominant U.S. or Chinese platform providers, for example.

Decentralized platform ecosystems are likely to produce a platform with governance that is independent of the initiating legal entity, i.e., the foundation. Therefore, a decentralized platform ecosystem can be initiated by entities that are interested in launching an underlying foundation – an innovation platform meant to accommodate a plethora of use cases from the most diverse industries. Furthermore, instead of internal business cases, platform initiation may be incentivized by the issuance of tokens and the prospect of raising token prices as soon as they are traded on cryptocurrency exchanges. Tokens are, thus, not only an indispensable decision-making tool but also a central incentive mechanism.

It is, thus, all the more critical for democratized platform ecosystem projects to carefully think about governance from the very beginning. Understanding the DLTs' potential and the importance of ecosystem governance is paramount for the project's success. Only when such projects take a holistic view of governance and technology, democratized platform ecosystems can realize their full potential and enable a new wave of economic and social value creation.

Section B:
Business Perspectives on Ecosystem Governance

Multidextrous Strategy – How to Excel in Platform-driven Ecosystems

Michael Hilb

Abstract
Platform-driven ecosystems follow their own rules. The article explains these rules and presents four key principles that guide strategic moves in platform-driven ecosystems, i.e. from linear to circular value creation, from centralized to distributed governance, from the five forces to platform forces, and, finally, from strategies to stratagems. By shedding light on the eleven platform stratagems, the article provides a strategy framework for identifying the strategic actions of other actors and planning one's own strategic moves. Finally, it proposes the concept of multidextrous strategy as a meta-capability that should be mastered by any strategy leader who wants to excel in ecosystems.

Author
Michael Hilb is founder and CEO of DBP Group and sits on several boards, such as Klingelnberg, Sigvaris Group, or the International Board Foundation. As a Titular Professor at the University of Fribourg, he teaches strategy, entrepreneurship, and corporate governance at universities in Asia and Europe. Michael Hilb graduated from the University of St. Gallen with an MSc and a PhD, was a Visiting Fellow at Harvard University and INSEAD, and completed several executive education programs at leading business schools.

1 Introduction

As more sectors transform from vendor-centric models to user-centric ecosystems, business leaders must decide whether to shape their company's future under these new conditions or be shaped by them. The transformation they must confront is not just about making the right move in a game with known rules, but often about learning a new game with new rules. Knowing these rules, and learning how to apply them, is therefore the key to success in this game.

What are the key rules of the game? We see four key principles guiding every strategic move into or onto platform-driven ecosystems:
1. From linear to circular value creation
2. From centralized to distributed governance
3. From the five forces to the platform forces
4. From strategies to stratagems

2 From Linear to Circular Value Creation

The first and fundamental rule to apply is to take a circular perspective to value creation as opposed to a linear approach. The linear perspective on value creation, which prevailed for a long time, assumed economic value creation as a sequential process along the value chain. Companies positioned themselves in the value chain, either through one or several stages, and focused on downward and upward relationships, i.e., with their suppliers and customers. As highlighted by Ramírez and Mannervik (2016), value creation was mainly additive, i.e., each actor used the components provided by its supplier as the basis for its output, e.g., a component or a final product. Those companies that managed this process more effectively and efficiently than their competitors gained power and, thereby, profitability.

While this logic still holds for many manufacturers, the balance of power shifted when new types of players entered the scene, offering a more efficient and effective way to market making, i.e., allocating resources, goods, services, and capital: digital platforms. Because of their ability to connect many more potential buyers and sellers than was previously possible for any one company, even the largest, they were able to better match supply and demand (Parker, Van Alstyne, and Choudary 2016). These companies benefited from and leveraged new technologies that were increasingly becoming available at a lower cost, i.e., the 3Cs, computing, connectivity, and cognitive performance through artificial intelligence. This changed the strategic challenge of the companies.

As a result, companies began to realize that their greatest challenge is not primarily competition, but rather their ability to cooperate and compete at the same time, or to co-operate, as suggested by Brandenburger and Nalebuff (2021). In this context, it is about being part of a larger network of firms, some of which are competitors, collaborators, or complementors. Consequently, innovation becomes more open (Chesbrough, 2003) and the rules of the network economy complement those of economies of scale (Williamson and De Meyer 2020). What remains, however, is a shared value proposition (Adner 2017). This has clear implications for the notion of industry and strategy, as Ramírez and Mannervik (2016, 32) note: "The increasingly outdated notion of 'industry' unduly and artificially narrows the frame the strategist uses; and thus the strategic focus of attention with regard to opportunities and threats."

In summary, the value creation logic is changing from a linear, one-dimensional perspective to a circular, multidimensional approach. This requires a multidextrous mindset.

3 From Centralized to Distributed Governance

The new economic realities are also reflected in the changing governance logic: from purely centralized, hierarchical governance to more distributed, shared governance. This is a direct consequence of the nature of ecosystems, as defined by Jacobides, Cennamo, and Gawer (2018, 2264): "An ecosystem is a set of actors with varying degrees of multilateral, nongeneric complementarities that are not fully hierarchically controlled." While decentralized value architectures have existed in the past, they have usually been influenced directly or indirectly by individual organizations.

If we combine the changes in value creation with those in governance logic, we can distinguish between four different value creation logics:

- **Value Chain:** The Value Chain architecture proposed by Porter (1980) assumes a linear logic in which firms seek to extend control downstream, i.e., to suppliers, and upstream, i.e., to distributors. Industry consolidation is an important means of extending control, either by buying out other firms or by increasing bargaining power over them.
- **Value Network:** The Value Network architecture as introduced by Brandenburger and Nalebuff (1996) still assumes a linear value creation logic but takes into account a distributed control logic that leads to co-opetitive relationships between actors, as a business partner can be both a competitor and a complementor.

- **Value Hub:** By contrast, Value Hubs assume a circular value creation logic driven by a central "platform" as proposed by Gawer and Cusumano (2002) or Parker, Van Alstyne, and Choudary (2016). The Value Hub, i.e., the platform, is at the center of the value creation mechanism and seeks to exert influence to maximize interdependencies and thereby optimize its value.
- **Value Web:** Finally, the Value Web architecture shares the circular value creation logic of the Value Hub, but also assumes a distributed governance logic, i.e., without a central platform that attempts to exert control over the various actors. In this approach, the different actors agree on the terms of a common governance to control the value creation activities.

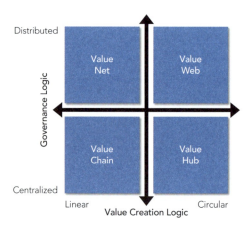

Exhibit 1: Value Architectures | valuearchitectures.com

While all four value creation architectures can be observed, and will continue to be so in the future, the value creation potential among them differs over time. While in the past, well-organized Value Chains embedded in Value Webs were the most profitable, many of the most capitalized companies today are Value Hubs. Only the future will reveal whether Value Webs will replace Value Hubs as the most profitable value architecture. Therefore, companies must be well versed in operating across all value architectures.

4 From the Five Forces to the Platform Forces

This change in the relevance of value architectures, and the increasing relevance of circular value creation logic, has direct implications for strategy. As outlined above, the focus is shifting beyond competition (Porter 1980) and co-opetition (Brandenburger and Nalebuff 1996) to platforms (Gawer and Cusumano 2002 or Parker, Van Alstyne, and Choudary 2016). Hence, we will move mentally from the five forces to the platform forces. What are they, and how do they differ from the five forces?

The key difference is the importance of organizational linkages in the platform logic (Gulati 1999). While the positioning of individual actors relative to others is still important, the relationships between them matter just as much. The five forces are as follows (Hilb 2020):

1. **Platform Orchestrator:** The Platform Orchestrator is at the center of an ecosystem and forms the connective bond for all players. It manages and controls all data and information flows.
2. **Platform Feeder:** The Platform Feeder provides the inputs for any transaction or transfer, e.g., goods, services, and information, to any other party. It considers the Platform Orchestrator as its channel to connect with the Platform User.
3. **Platform User:** The Platform User views the Platform Orchestrator as the source of goods, services, or information. It appreciates the variety of opportunities that would not be enjoyed if it had to interact with every individual platform player.
4. **Platform Aggregator:** The Platform Aggregator helps Platform Feeders and Platform Users navigate the growing universe of platforms, select the most appropriate platforms, and adapt partner strategies in an ever-changing environment.
5. **Platform Enhancer:** The Platform Enhancer offers additional services or products that facilitate the transaction and interaction relationship between the other platform players. Their offer is usually closely linked to individual transactions and interactions.

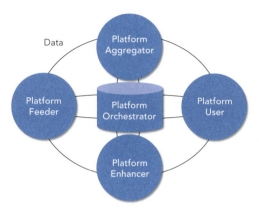

Exhibit 2: Platform Forces | platformforces.com

The three shifts described above have direct implications for the nature of competition and collaboration. First, the circular nature of value creation presupposes the simultaneous application of a combination of different strategic logics, i.e., competition and collaboration. Second, the trend toward distributed leadership implies a division of influence and responsibility, but also a limitation of strategic autonomy. Third, companies will have to choose not only between multiple ecosystems, but also between different roles within them, i.e., among the platform forces.

Therefore, these transitions directly affect the concept of competitive advantage, or as Jacobides (2019, 11) summarizes, "Competing is increasingly about identifying new ways to collaborate and connect rather than simply offering alternative value propositions." Are we observing the end of competitive advantage, as suggested by McGrath (2013), or simply a new application of Teece's (2007) dynamic capabilities?

5 From Strategies to Stratagems

While the nature of competitive advantage may change, the central role of strategy will remain. However, the way strategies are developed and applied is likely to change. Strategies will be more ephemeral, will need to be more adaptive, and will therefore need to be developed in a more agile manner. Therefore, we may no longer even speak of 'strategy' but rather of 'stratagem,' defined as "a carefully planned way of achieving or dealing with something, often involving a trick" (Cambridge Dictionary, 2021), whereby we would define 'trick' as a clever way of interacting with other players to achieve a goal.

What are the stratagems for succeeding in ecosystems? To outline the option space, it can be useful to look at the company lifecycle and business model. In that context we can distinguish between three types of companies (Hilb 2020): the upstart, the incumbent, and the Platform Orchestrator.

While upstarts are usually well positioned to play the vertical game, i.e., take on the role of Platform Aggregator, Orchestrator, or Enhancer, as they are not locked into old thought patterns and relationships, incumbents that have grown in a more linear value creation logic may have an advantage to play the horizontal game in platform-driven ecosystems, i.e., evolve as Platform Feeders and Users. Finally, Platform Orchestrators are well positioned to move in all four directions. What are the stratagems in play?

Upstart Plays

1. **Connector Play:** With the increasing number of ecosystems and players within them, there is a need to provide independent guidance and navigation. New players are well positioned to act as aggregators and help provide clarity and orientation in the world of ecosystems.
2. **Disruptor Play:** Even disruptors risk being disrupted. Upstart companies are ideally placed to challenge an existing platform by offering a novel experience or a superior coordination model, such as distributed governance.
3. **Micro-solution Play:** Most upstarts find their white space in developing a new application embedded into a platform that helps enhance its offerings and experience. Micro-solution plays can benefit from an existing network, but platform dependency may also limit its option space.

Incumbent Plays

4. **Channel Play:** The obvious way for any player to leverage ecosystems is to try to capture distribution channels and reach as many players as possible to market and sell their products and services.
5. **Emulator Play:** Many established players try to emulate the strategies of existing platforms to become Platform Orchestrators themselves. As logical as this may sound to many players, the path usually proves difficult. Instead of trying to emulate an existing platform, it may be smarter to team up with other players to form an alliance.
6. **Optimizer Play:** As with the channel play, most companies see benefits in using ecosystems as a sourcing option, whether for goods, information, or data. This usually leads to better prices and optimized results and helps to identify new potential business partners.

Platform Orchestrator Plays

7. **Value Capture Play:** Platform Orchestrators have the most opportunities to position themselves in ecosystems because they are in a comfortable starting position. One obvious choice is to move from connecting sellers with buyers to selling products on their own. This allows the orchestrator to capture more of the value of a transaction.

8. **Absorber Play:** Another strategy often chosen by Platform Orchestrators to expand their reach is to become an Aggregator and thereby absorb the business of competing platforms. This is often done through acquisitions but can also be achieved in a greenfield approach.

9. **Gatekeeper Play:** One way for digital platforms to grow in the analog world is to get closer to end users, in channels they may not yet control. Since in many cases the middlemen remain between the platforms and the users, platform orchestrators may be well positioned to replace the middleman altogether.

10. **Infrastructure Play:** Another area where Platform Orchestrators can find future growth is expansion into infrastructure, i.e., becoming a Platform Enhancer. Moves into infrastructure are often the result of a lack of technology or services available in the quality and quantity needed or may even become a competitive advantage.

11. **Replicator Play:** Finally, Platform Orchestrators can effectively replicate the platform model in another ecosystem. Because they have the experience, technology, and business acumen, which are required to be a successful Platform Orchestrator, they can easily apply those capabilities in other ecosystems.

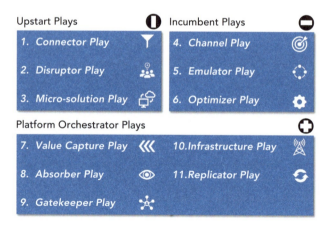

Exhibit 3: Platform Stratagems | platformstratagems.com

6 Conclusions

We have discussed four major shifts that companies need to master to lead successfully in ecosystems: From linear to circular value creation, from centralized to distributed governance, from the five forces to the platform forces, and, finally, from strategies to stratagems. These shifts not only present a major change and challenge for organizations, but also put pressure on the organization to navigate a multidimensional option space that requires multidextrous strategies and governance approaches to succeed. In this context, the main challenge for decision makers is to consider simultaneous options along four dimensions:

1. **Which ecosystems?** Since most companies can be a part of various ecosystems, decision makers need to prioritize and evaluate the relevance of each one. The assessment must be based on both the capabilities of the business and the future attractiveness of the ecosystem.
2. **Which roles?** All five roles that companies can play in ecosystems require certain skills, but also deliver advantages and disadvantages under their respective conditions. Companies need to decide which roles they want to play now and in the future. In many cases, they must choose multiple roles simultaneously and adjust their choices as ecosystems evolve.
3. **Which stratagems?** Once the positioning is clear, at least in the short term, organizations need to know what strategic options they have available, i.e., what stratagems they should pursue. Again, different stratagems can work and may need to be adjusted as the game evolves.
4. **Which behaviors?** Finally, organizations should be clear about how they want to interact with the other players in the ecosystem, competitively or collaboratively. Since relationships with most actors will proceed in both directions, organizations must not only be able to behave in different ways, but also know when to behave in which specific way.

In conclusion, success in ecosystems requires a multidextrous mind and skill set. Multidexterity, however, does not mean doing everything, for any reason, at all times. Rather, organizations should develop the necessary capabilities and be clear about when to use them, either individually or together with other players, as required.

Literature

Adner, R. (2017). Ecosystem as structure: An actionable construct for strategy. Journal of management, 43(1), 39-58.

Brandenburger, A., & Nalebuff, B. (2021). The rules of co-opetition. Harvard Business Review, 1, 48-57.

Brandenburger, A., & Nalebuff, B. (1996). Co-opetition. Doubleday, New York, NY.

Cambridge Dictionary (2021). Stratagem, https://dictionary.cambridge.org

Chesbrough, H. W. (2003). Open innovation: The new imperative for creating and profiting from technology. Harvard Business Press.

Gawer, A., & Cusumano, M. A. (2002). Platform leadership: How Intel, Microsoft, and Cisco drive industry innovation (Vol. 5, pp. 29-30). Boston, MA: Harvard Business School Press.

Gulati, R. (1999). Network location and learning: The influence of network resources and firm capabilities on alliance formation. Strategic management journal, 20(5), 397-420.

Hilb, M. (2020). Cracking the collaboration codes – How to succeed in ecosystems. In Governance of Ventures, Hilb, M. 97-106. Haupt, Bern, CH.

Jacobides, M. G. (2019). In the ecosystem economy, what's your strategy? Harvard Business Review, 97(5), 128-137.

Jacobides, M. G., Cennamo, C., & Gawer, A. (2018). Towards a theory of ecosystems. Strategic Management Journal, 39(8), 2255-2276.

McGrath, R. G. (2013). The end of competitive advantage: How to keep your strategy moving as fast as your business. Harvard Business Review Press.

Minnaar, J. (2020). The age of community capitalism. In: Ecosystem Inc.: Understanding, harnessing and developing organizational ecosystems. Crainer. S. Thinkers50, London, UK. 120-132.

Parker, G. G., Van Alstyne, M. W., & Choudary, S. P. (2016). Platform revolution: How networked markets are transforming the economy and how to make them work for you. WW Norton & Company.

Porter, M. E. (1980). Competitive strategy. The Free Press, New York, NY.

Ramírez, R, & Mannervik, U. (2016). Strategy for a networked world. World Scientific Publishing Company, Singapore, SG.

Teece, D. J. (2007). Explicating dynamic capabilities: the nature and microfoundations of (sustainable) enterprise performance. Strategic Management Journal, 28(13), 1319-1350.

Williamson, P. J., & De Meyer, A. (2020). Ecosystem edge: Sustaining competitiveness in the face of disruption. Stanford University Press.

How to Successfully Launch a Digital Ecosystem Business – The Role of Communications

Karin Taheny

Abstract
More than half of ecosystems never take off and get beyond the startup phase. During this first step toward a sustainable business, most ecosystem companies find themselves in a chicken-or-egg situation where they must simultaneously convince both potential customers and (the right) partners to engage and invest in an unproven business opportunity. This requires careful planning and execution of communication activities from both partners and potential customers.

Author
Karin Taheny is a member of the executive team at Dept Agency. Before joining Dept, she worked for Omnicom Media Group and Google in Switzerland, Ireland and the US. She holds a master's degree in economics from the University of Zurich. She is a member of the board of directors of several companies and a part-time lecturer at the University of Applied Sciences (HWZ) in Zurich, Switzerland.

1 Defeating the Odds of Failure

Studies show that most ecosystems fail. In fact, only 15 % of ecosystems survive and thrive in the long run (Reeves et al. 2019). One aspect that many of the successful ventures have in common is that they are either digitally enabled or fully digital, such as Open Table (restaurant reservations), Google Nest (smart home), or Ping An Group (financial products and services). Driven by innovation, digital ecosystems could unlock up to $100 trillion in value for businesses and society at large by 2028, provide myriad opportunities for new companies to penetrate traditional industries, and offer complex and customizable product-service bundles to increasingly demanding customers (Jacobides 2019 or Lyman, Ref, and Wright 2018).

When establishing an ecosystem over the long term, there are three critical windows for success (Reeves et al. 2019): capture market share, evolve the model and secure market leadership.

Looking at the three windows that can determine the success or failure of an ecosystem, the first is by far the most challenging. Over 50 % of ecosystems never take off. Given the often significant initial investment required to launch a business, it is worth looking at these challenges and how they can be overcome (Reeves et al. 2019 and Pidun, Reeves, and Schlüssler 2020).

2 The Chicken and the Egg

During this first step toward a sustainable business, most ecosystem companies find themselves in a chicken-or-egg situation where they must simultaneously convince both potential customers and (the right) ecosystem partners to engage and invest in an unproven business opportunity (Pidun, Reeves, and Schlüssler 2020).

On the one hand, gaining customers and demonstrating demand for the business makes joining the ecosystem more attractive to potential partners. In addition, a critical number of customers and customer interactions/transactions must be achieved to make the business profitable and lay the foundation for further growth. However, since most ecosystem solutions only come to life when ecosystem partners are involved and contribute to the business, there may be no business if partners are not convinced first (Sengupta et al. 2019b, 9).

Exhibit 1: Ecosystem dynamics

The only way to be successful in the launch phase is to address both sides of the equation synchronously and at high speed. Achieving this requires careful planning and tailored communications to get both sides on board. Companies that fail to master this task are unlikely to make it past the launch phase (Reeves et al. 2019).

3 Three Steps to Effective Communication with Ecosystem Partners

3.1 Create Value for Stakeholders

In an attempt to solve the chicken-and-egg paradox, many ecosystems offer significant discounts to customers in order to quickly gain market share (Sengupta et al. 2019a). As a result, this means that profitability for ecosystem partners can be delayed (Reeves et al. 2019). To overcome this period of low revenue, orchestrators need to ensure that ecosystem participation provides value to their partners now and inspires them to stay on board for the long term (Jacobides 2019). The value does not necessarily have to be monetary but can also be access (initially free) to technology, knowledge or data. OpenTable, for example, began by offering restaurants a set of software tools that replaced their manual booking process. This led to a number of high-profile restaurants joining the platform, making it attractive for customers to use OpenTable services (Pidun, Reeves, and Schlüssler 2020). Knowing what is important and beneficial to partners allows for tailored communication and building long-term, stable relationships.

3.2 Assign Roles and Set Expectations

Given the highly dynamic nature of ecosystems, it is important to remain consistent in your communication with the partners involved. Take the time to create a RACI matrix together, primarily by consulting with key partners or representatives of a stakeholder group. The acronym RACI stands for the four roles stakeholders can take and is commonly used to define roles and responsibilities during a project with higher complexity and a larger number of stakeholders, i.e. Responsible (stakeholder who is responsible for communication), Accountable (stakeholder who is accountable and has yes/no veto power), Consult (stakeholder who should be consulted before communication but does not have veto power), and Inform (stakeholder who simply needs to be informed).

This second step of effective communication with partners should be closely aligned with their interests and expected benefits, as described above in Section 1. This exercise may seem excessive in the rush to market, but it is extremely valuable. Not only does it ensure that expectations are clear, but it also establishes communication standards for later phases (Lang et al. 2019). Ensuring that partners feel included gives them an active and engaged role in the journey to success (Kantor 2018). Consistent communication leads to trust and robust relationships-even when things don't go according to plan.

3.3 Establish Appropriate Communication Channels

Within an ecosystem, there is a high need for coordination among stakeholders (Pidun, Reeves, and Schlüssler 2020). Knowing what content needs to be communicated to partners and what roles are associated with that communication can effectively streamline efforts and resources. Orchestrators need to ensure that they put the right communication systems in place to foster this dialogue. One of the greatest strengths of an ecosystem is the diversity of internal and external stakeholders. Communication is key to getting the most out of this setup and sparking new ideas and positive outcomes (Groysberg 2012). Channel selection may need to be adjusted as the organization and partnership evolve. Some channels to consider:

- Personal exchange in the group (events, roundtables, networking events)
- Personal individual exchange (personal meetings, phone calls)
- Chat system for ad-hoc communication
- Email groups (built around topics/interests)
- Knowledge sharing platform (intranet, webinars, training)

Be sure to adjust frequency and content to partners' needs to avoid information overload (Bühlmann 2018). Establishing the right communication channels early on can help manage partner interest over time and secure long-term leadership.

A successful ecosystem business is built on strong partnerships but will not be a thriving business without customers. We have learned that both sides need to be addressed at the same time. We also know that speed is critical.

Ecosystem solutions usually emerge when partners join. Consequently, this also means that there is no complete value proposition when first approaching customers. One way to increase the chances of a successful launch is to start with a Minimum Viable Ecosystem (MVE), where the focus is entirely on the core transaction or hook product that is best suited to attract customers quickly without overwhelming them with too much complexity (Sengupta et al. 2019a). As mentioned earlier, many ecosystem companies choose to subsidize this hook product for the customer side in order to quickly gain market share – for example, through an "introductory offer" or a "free trial." Unfortunately, this method often results in comparatively low customer retention (Sengupta et al. 2019a). Companies face the challenge of following up on these initial contacts with customers and building long-term relationships. A structured approach to customer communication can help guide potential customers through this journey.

4 Three Steps to Successful Communication with Ecosystem Customers

4.1 Communicate along the Decision-making Process

If you want to introduce your business to potential customers, a detailed marketing plan is key. There are many models that can help with a structured approach to this topic. One model is the See-Think-Do-Care model by Kaushik (2015). It is based on the idea that potential customers have different needs and questions depending on where they are in their decision-making process:
- See: The customer has never heard of your product
- Think: The customer is interested in learning more about your product
- Do: The customer wants to buy your product
- Maintenance: The customer has bought your product at least once

Each phase must be addressed with the right content and via the right channels. In the initial launch, it can be assumed that most customers can be assigned to the "seeing" phase, in which they have not yet interacted with the solution or the company. Getting this initial phase right is especially important for ecosystems that offer innovative solutions that require explanation or training. It can be useful to provide explainer videos and, in any case, have high-quality customer service to remove hurdles for potential customers. Speed is key, if customers don't understand the offer, they won't stick with it.

4.2 Partner in Communication

In most cases, communication is managed centrally by the ecosystem's orchestrator. However, one advantage of ecosystems is that there is the opportunity to benefit from the reputation and even the customer list of their partners (always in compliance with data regulations, of course). For example, a joint effort by Alibaba Group and Bosch to refine customer data and segmentation in 2017 resulted in three times higher customer acquisition conversion rates for Bosch in China (Sengupta et al. 2019a).

If an ecosystem partner of strategic importance already has a strong and relevant customer base, the initial launch communication should be conducted jointly. At the same time, the message must be coordinated in terms of content and timing to achieve the best results and present a consistent image to the potential customer.

4.3 Maintain Connection after the First Interest

Once customers have engaged with the hook product, the challenge is to retain them and develop customer loyalty (Sengupta et al. 2019a). Especially when an innovative solution is presented to the market, it is critical to establish a strong feedback system that allows the company to develop and expand the offering based on the customer experience. By listening to customers, improvements can be made to offer frictionless experiences that reduce customer loss and churn (Sengupta et al. 2019b). From a marketing perspective, it is advisable to use multidimensional data for precision marketing (e.g., customer behavior, purchase behavior, demographics, etc.). For example, customers who have previously shown interest in the solution can be retargeted with a complementary product or service that offers a greater margin for the ecosystem business.

It is not easy to successfully launch an ecosystem. Communication can make the difference between success and failure of a promising ecosystem. Make this practice a top priority.

Case: Switzerland Global Enterprise

Switzerland Global Enterprise (S-GE) is the official Swiss export and investment promotion organization with offices throughout Switzerland and in 31 countries. The company has been mandated by the Swiss government (State Secretariat for Economic Affairs SECO) to promote exports since 1927 and supports Swiss SMEs in their international business and helps innovative foreign companies to establish themselves in Switzerland. To this end, Switzerland Global Enterprise works with a unique network of national and global partners and assumes the role of an orchestrator. In this role, it does not compete with private providers and only provides services where an affordable and suitable offer for SMEs is not available on the market.

As such, S-GE pools the expertise of its partners and connects customers with the right buyers, experts, partners and authorities from around the world. S-GE also connects its customers with each other so they can share their expertise. To coordinate the work of the Swiss and leverage synergies in a targeted manner, Switzerland Global Enterprise uses a range of digital and non-digital channels for efficient and dialog-oriented communication. Some examples include a virtual LinkedIn community where relevant updates and curated content are shared, or annual physical meetings of relevant stakeholder groups to foster knowledge sharing and build connections. A growing range of digital and web-based sharing and collaboration opportunities are deployed to best reflect the needs of ecosystem partners and SME customers, such as a networking and exchange platform for companies in the cleantech sector.

Literature

Bühlmann, B. (2018). Managing digital transformation at the board level. M. Hilb. Governance of Digitalization, 2nd edition, 28-34. Haupt, Bern.

Groysberg, B., & Slind, M. (2012). The silent killer of big companies. Harvard Business Review, 90(10).

Jacobides, M. G. (2019). In the ecosystem economy, what's your strategy? Harvard Business Review, 97(5), 128-137.

Kantor, B. (2018). The RACI matrix: Your blueprint for project success. CIO Online. January 30. https://www.cio.com/article/2395825/project-management-how-to-design-a-successful-raci-project-plan.html

Kaushik, A. (2015). See, think, care winning combo: Content + marketing + measurement! July 6. https://www.kaushik.net/avinash/see-think-do-care-win-content-marketing-measurement

Lang, N., von Szczepanski, K., & Wurzer, C. (2019). The emerging art of ecosystem management. BCG Henderson Institute.

Lyman, M., Ref, R., & Wright, O. (2018). Cornerstone of future growth: Ecosystems. Accenture Strategy.

Pidun, U., Reeves, M., & Schlüssler, M. (2020). Why do most business ecosystems fail? BCG Henderson Institute.

Reeves, M., Lotan, H., Legrand, J., & Jacobides, M. G. (2019). How business ecosystems rise (and often fall). MIT Sloan Management Review, 60(4), 1-6.

Sengupta, J., HV, V., Chung, V., Ji, X., Ng, E., Xiao, L., Koh, K. & Chen, C. (2019a). The ecosystem playbook: Winning in a world of ecosystems. McKinsey Report.

Sengupta, J., HV, V., Dietz, M., Chung, V., Ji, X., Xiao, L., & Li, L. (2019b). How the best companies create value from their ecosystems. McKinsey Report.

Section C:
Organizational Perspectives on Ecosystem Governance

The Power of Power in Shaping Organizations

Michael Hilb

Abstract

There is much talk about new organizational forms and paradigm shifts in organizational design. This article argues that what often appears new has its antecedents and is more a function of ever-changing conditions. By analyzing the changing faces of organizations along two dimensions, the boundaries and the functioning of organizations, the article establishes a cyclical model of organizations informed by the search for a balance of power and governance. It presents eleven governance cycles that help to understand the dynamic nature of organizations. The article concludes with a strong call to actively shape organizations in creative ways based on a thorough understanding of the conditions and options that influence organizational dynamics.

Author

Michael Hilb is founder and CEO of DBP Group and sits on several boards, such as Klingelnberg, Sigvaris Group, or the International Board Foundation. As a Titular Professor at the University of Fribourg, he teaches strategy, entrepreneurship, and corporate governance at universities in Asia and Europe. Michael Hilb graduated from the University of St. Gallen with an MSc and a PhD, was a Visiting Fellow at Harvard University and INSEAD, and completed several executive education programs at leading business schools.

1 The Changing Faces of Organizations

1.1 The Two Dimensions of the Organization

The organization, defined as institutionalized collective action, is the dominant face of society and the economy. Whatever the desired outcome of the collective action may be, i.e. financial returns ('money'), political power ('might') or thought leadership ('mind') (Casas, Hilb, and Lim 2021), the role of institutions is critical. While corporations dominate the economic value creation machine ('money'), academic, civic, and religious institutions play an important role in shaping ideas ('mind'), and political parties and government institutions are critical in shaping public decisions ('might'). Although institutions are shaped by individuals and, in many cases, individuals embody organizations, e.g., the founder, the CEO, or the political leader, it is the institution that usually outlives the individuals and where value is eventually created or destroyed.

While the importance of institutions can be observed throughout human history, some of the characteristics have changed. In this context, two dimensions of change stand out:

- **The boundary of the organization:** Which activities are bundled within an organization or in cooperation with other institutions or persons? Here we can distinguish between market-based and decision-based modes of governance.
- **The functioning of the organization:** How are the activities within an institution organized and controlled? Here we can distinguish between hierarchy-based and democracy-based modes of governance.

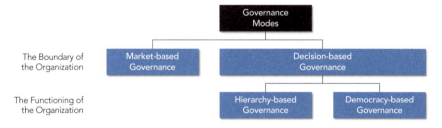

Exhibit 1: Governance Modes | governancemodes.com

1.2 The Outside View – The Boundary of the Organization

The delineation of organizations has been extensively discussed in various academic fields, such as sociology, economics, and law. Sociologist Weber (1922) recognized the importance of institutions as a means of collective action and explained their existence in terms of the superior power of collective over individual action.

Economist Williamson (1979) provided an alternative perspective, positing transaction costs as a key factor in determining the boundaries of the firm. According to his argument, economic decision makers must decide whether to buy a product in the market or hire employees to produce it internally. In making the decision, they must consider both price and the costs associated with transactions, such as controlling quality and the costs of hiring and training employees. His theory is helpful in explaining corporate decisions to in- and outsource activities.

Finally, from a legal perspective, the most important determinant of institutional boundaries is liability (Berle and Means 1933). Since institutions are juridical persons, they offer the possibility of limiting the liability of those involved in certain activities. At the same time, the decisions that lead to these activities must follow well-established procedures and be justified to underscore that individuals are acting in their best interests. A basic dichotomy emerges in all three perspectives: Market-based vs. decision-based modes of governance.

1.3 The Inside View – The Functioning of the Organization

Even more attention than the question of the optimal boundary of organizations has been given to the effective functioning of the organization. Here, the discussion revolves around the optimal positioning on a continuum between bottom-up and top-down decision-making, between influence- and command-and-control-driven leadership cultures, or between hierarchy- and democracy-based governance models.

The optimal set-up is not only determined by efficiency considerations, but also by philosophical values. In all three areas addressed, there is competition between leadership modes. While political ('might'), academic and spiritual ('mind') organizations tend to use democracy-based governance modes, or at least pretend to do so, commercial institutions ('money') often follow a more hierarchy-based approach.

Nonetheless, alternative approaches are often proposed at all three levels, be it the concept of benevolent dictatorship or holacracy. It could even be argued that all modes of governance are constantly being challenged.

1.4 The Governance Modes Under Scrutiny

The questioning of the dominant mode of governance is neither new nor likely to be discontinued. On the contrary, this debate is of great importance for institutional design. Although some of the arguments challenging the status quo appear to be new, counter-arguments to the three main modes of governance have a long tradition.

Challenges to the market as a mode of governance originate not only on ideological grounds, i.e., questioning the capitalist nature of markets as a legitimate mode of governance (Marx, 1867), but also on efficiency grounds. As outlined above, Williamson (1979) sees limitations to markets as transaction costs may outweigh price efficiency effects. Others emphasize that the increasing dynamics of market conditions make it impossible to rely solely on competitive market mechanisms, but rather call for a combination of competitive market and cooperative nonmarket governance mechanisms, i.e., co-opetition (Nalebuff and Brandenburger 1996).

The governance mode of hierarchy is not only challenged by market purists as outlined above, but also by those who see operational constraints in a top-down culture and the need to move away from a command-and-control approach to grant more autonomy and decision-making power to individuals and teams in organizations. If the argument is taken to the extreme of abolishing hierarchy, concepts such as Holacracy (Robertson 2007) or related frameworks such as Wirearchy (Husband 2015), Podularity (Gray and Vander Wal 2014), or Unboss (Kolind and Bøtter 2012) emerge. They all argue for less hierarchical and more democratic governance of organizations.

While democracy as a mode of government may seem like an obvious counter-proposal to the limitations of hierarchy, it has been challenged since its inception. Unlike opponents who propose hierarchy as an alternative, some challengers see the solution in sociocracy. The main argument against democracy in its purest form, i.e., full and equal decision-making power by all members, is based on two arguments. First, they doubt its feasibility, i.e., lack of time and knowledge, and the danger of manipulation, i.e., demagoguery or the formation of undemocratic alliances as a consequence. Instead, intellectuals in the 19th century, such as Comte (1851) or Ward (1893), proposed the concept of sociocracy, which allows decision-making by different groups at different levels in institutions. Others, such as Priest and Bockelbrink (2015), have taken the original concept and adapted it to contemporary conditions.

How can the longevity of the two modes of governance and their challenges be explained simultaneously? We believe that introducing the concept of power cannot only help explain this ambiguity but will also be helpful to better debate the future of organizations and discuss its implications.

1.5 Enter Power

The relevance of power in shaping organizations is nothing new. Machiavelli (1532) was not the first author to recognize the role of power both in terms of leadership and in shaping the organization to cement power. Modern management scholars such as Pfeffer (1994) have taken up the concept and introduced their own school of thought in strategy, the power school (Ahlstrand, Lampel, and Mintzberg 2001). It argues that understanding the power structure is critical to comprehending, but also driving, business transformation. As is typical in any time of disruption, whether political, economic, or technological, the power structure also seems to be disrupted. While some refer to this as the emergence of a 'new power' (Heimans and Timms 2018), others view the change in power structures as indicative of the prevalence of power as an eternal factor shaping society and the economy, with direct implications for how organizations operate and function (Pfeffer 1994).

We sympathize with the latter position and consider power as a key factor to better understand the choice of governance modes. More specifically, we see governance mode choice as related to power structure. How is power related to governance?

2 Power and Governance – Towards a Balance?

To relate power and governance, we assume a correlation between power concentration and how it is reflected in the chosen governance mode by conceptualizing how centralized governance is. The combination of these two dimensions provides an indication of how the concentration of power is reflected in the governance model chosen. In this sense, if we assume a direct correlation between power and governance, two states would result. In the case of high power concentration, we would see more centralized governance models, while in the case of distributed power, we would experience more decentralized governance models.

This aligns very well with Ferguson's (2019) characterization of Square and Tower structures. In his historical analysis of the prevalence of power structures, he found that periods during which power was expressed in centralized ways were followed by periods in which more bottom-up networks prevailed. He thus identified not only the two archetypes in history, but also a pattern of succession. Therefore, can we assume that the two phases identified indicate a natural equilibrium?

We believe that the relationship between power and governance may be driven by a natural search for equilibrium but may be quite unbalanced along the way. Therefore, we also assume the existence of two other potential correlations, i.e., high power concentration but use of more decentralized governance models and high-power distribution and more centralized governance models. Based on this assumption, we extend the perspective of Ferguson (2019) by adding more governance models, the Souk and the Fortress. Therefore, we will distinguish four governance models:

1. **Square:** This describes a governance model in which power is distributed among participants without a centralized governance structure. Therefore, decisions are made informally, mostly on an ad-hoc basis.
2. **Souk:** The Souk governance model is characterized by deliberately decentralized leadership. While power is concentrated among a few and the powerful could claim decision-making power for themselves, they prefer to delegate it to the periphery, which enables agility and flexibility.
3. **Tower:** In the Tower governance model, power is concentrated among a few who also exercise it in a centralized manner. As a result, the organization is run in a hierarchical manner with key decisions concentrated at the top.
4. **Fortress:** Finally, the Fortress governance model describes a state in which legitimate power is widely distributed, but decision-makers cling to their decision-making power for lack of legitimacy. As a result, decisions must be enforced through fear and pressure, otherwise those who receive the orders may not follow.

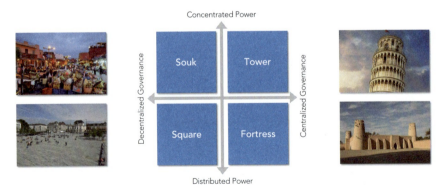

Exhibit 2: Governance Models | governancemodels.com

If we map the four governance models with the three governance modes presented earlier, we can see certain patterns. First, all four governance models have a primary correlation to one of the governance modes. Second, all governance models with the exception of the Fortress model appear to be a hybrid of at least two governance modes. We will see in the next section what this says about the sustainability of governance models.

Governance Modes	Governance Models			
	Square	Souk	Tower	Fortress
Democracy	X	x		
Market	x	X	x	
Hierarchy		x	X	X

X: primary correlation | x: secondary correlation

Exhibit 3: Linking governance models and governance modes

3 Power and Governance – A Dynamic Perspective

As mentioned above, we assume the four governance models to be temporary states in a never-ending search for equilibrium. Therefore, we will take a dynamic perspective on how the four models evolve and depend on each other.

3.1 The Evolution Governance Cycles

The four governance models are not only closely related but build on each other. They represent a logical evolution. We could even argue that they reflect the natural course of organizational evolution in the lifecycle of an organization.

1. **Rationalization:** Every organization begins in the Square mode when several people decide that they should align to achieve a particular result that could not be achieved by a single person alone. As a result, there is an inherent degree of power sharing and often little formalized leadership structure. As these organizations evolve, the concentration of power becomes apparent: new individuals joining the organization may have less power than the founders or, as in most cases, may be employees who are compensated for working on behalf of the institution. This also requires establishing internal rules and regulations while trying to maintain agility and flexibility. Thus, the organization streamlines and becomes what we call a Souk.

2. **Ratification:** While the Souk offers excellent conditions for generating new ideas and developing them into products, proposals and measures, the governance model reaches its limits when the focus shifts to external competition. Suddenly, it is not so much about innovation and creativity as it is about winning against other institutions. This often leads to a ratification of power and a more centralized governance model, i.e., the Tower. In this model, decisions are made by a small group of decision makers to ensure quick action and reaction when threatened or in attack mode.
3. **Resistance:** While the Tower governance model can be effective and beneficial to all participants in a competitive environment, there is a danger that decision makers become too accustomed to their privileged position and unwilling to share their decision-making power. Instead, they may focus their energy on cementing the status quo, resisting any opportunity, and preventing others from becoming decision makers. As a result, their leadership style can be likened to a Fortress whose main goal is to defend the status quo.
4. **Revolution:** If decision-makers cannot find a way to balance legitimate power and effective decision-making power, they will be forced into an even more defensive position. This often leads to further resistance from those who challenge the status quo. This vicious cycle is rarely broken, leading to open revolution. Those in the Fortress may be able to resist the revolutionary forces for a time but they are often defeated, creating the conditions for the Square governance model to prevail.

3.2 The Intervention Governance Cycles

Fortunately, not all organizational developments lead to disaster. Various intervention options exist along the way:

5. **Reorientation:** One way to keep the spirit of the Square governance model intact is to reorient and allow the emergence of new collaborative partnerships between the different parties. The shift between groups is largely driven by ever-changing needs and expectations.
6. **Recollection:** For the Souk model to endure, a constant reminder of the cultural rules is required. Since the shared leadership of the members of the Souk are the basic principles, they must be regularly reflected and acted upon.
7. **Rejuvenation:** If the guiding principles of the Souk prove too limiting, rethinking the Square governance model may be the solution. This rejuvenation of the original spirit can release the energy needed to ignite new ideas.

8. **Renovation:** A common intervention method for maintaining the Tower governance model is the renovation approach. While the underlying logic and structures are maintained, the detailed rules are updated and refreshed to better reflect the new realities.
9. **Renewal:** If the Tower governance model proves to be unfit for purpose, for example in times of dynamism and disruption, renewal may be necessary. This means questioning the tenant structure of the Tower organization and returning to the Souk structure.
10. **Retreat:** The behavior in the Fortress organization of resisting change can often be described as complete retreat. Those in power decide to bunker down in the Fortress, ignoring any call for change and trying to avoid the inevitable, i.e., revolution.
11. **Reform:** An alternative approach to avoiding the inevitable, for those trapped in the Fortress governance model, is reform, i.e., changing the rules and structures to regain credibility with those who hold ultimate power. This often requires a change in the parties holding power to make the changes credible.

In summary, the four governance evolutions and seven intervention cycles presented earlier can be depicted as follows:

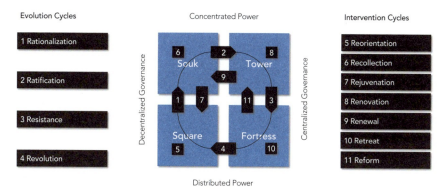

Exhibit 4: Governance Cycles | governancecycles.com

4 Implications

What can we learn from governance modes, models, and cycles? More importantly, how do these lessons inform our understanding of the future of the organization in times of rapid change?

First, we have seen that the three governance modes in their purest form usually do not lead to the desired outcomes, but rather need to be combined. Second, governance models should be viewed from an evolutionary perspective: They evolve over time in search of an equilibrium that they never achieve. Third, while there are natural evolutionary cycles of governance models, there are various interventions that can influence the evolution and allow the governance model to adapt to the purpose of the ever-changing conditions.

Since any organization today and in the future will be exposed to several such conditions, some of which are currently known while others have yet to be discovered, we can assume that any organization of the future is likely to be a combination of governance models that must change over time to be fit for purpose in the face of external demands and conditions.

For decision-makers, this means complexity on the one hand. On the other hand, it offers a wide range of opportunities to intervene and not only adapt the governance structure to its current purpose, but also to help make the organization truly future-proof.

Literature

Ahlstrand, B., Lampel, J., & Mintzberg, H. (2001). Strategy safari: A guided tour through the wilds of Strategic Management. Simon and Schuster, New York, NY.

Bengtsson, M., & Eriksson, J. W. J. (2010). Co-opetition dynamics–an outline for further inquiry. In: Competitiveness Review: An International Business Journal, 20(2), 194-214.

Berle, A. A., & Means, G. C. (1933). The modern corporation and private property. MacMillan, New York, NY.

Casas, T., Hilb, M., & Lim, A. (2021). Maintaining pole position along different paths – An examination of the quality of elites and their influence on value creation. The Business Times. March 23.

Comte, A. (1851). Système de politique positive : Discours préliminaire et l'introduction fondamentale (Vol. 1). Carilian-Goeury et Vor Dalmont, Paris, FR.

Ferguson, N. (2019). The square and the tower: Networks and power, from the freemasons to Facebook. Penguin Books, New York, NY.

Gray, D., & Vander Wal, T. (2014). The connected company. O'Reilly Media, New York, NY.

Heimans, J., & Timms, H. (2018). New power: How it's changing the 21st century-and why you need to know. MacMillan, New York, NY.

Husband, J. (2015). Wirearchy: Sketches for the future of work. Wirarchy Commons.

Kolind, L., & Bøtter, J. (2012). Unboss. Jyllands-Postens Forlag, Aarhus, DK.

Machiavelli, N. B. (1532). Il principe. Edited by Soares, S. M. (2005): MetaLibri, digital.

Marx, K. (1867). Das Kapital: Kritik der politischen Ökonomie. Band I-III. Verlag von Otto Meissner, Hamburg, DE.

Nalebuff, B. J., & Brandenburger, A. (1996). Co-opetition. HarperCollinsBusiness, London, UK.

Pfeffer, Jeffrey (1994). Managing with power: Politics and influence in organizations. Harvard Business Press, Boston, MA.

Priest, J., & Bockelbrink, B. (2015). Sociocracy 3.0. Sociocracy 3.0 Commons.

Robertson, B. J. (2007). Organization at the leading edge: Introducing Holacracy. Integral Leadership Review, 7(3), 1-13.

Ward, L. F (1893). Chapter XXXVIII: Sociocracy. In: The psychic factors of civilization. 311–331. Ginn & Company, Boston, MA.

Weber, M. (1922). Wirtschaft und Gesellschaft, Mohr-Siebeck, Tübingen, DE.

Williamson, O. E. (1979). Transaction-cost economics: the governance of contractual relations. The journal of Law and Economics, 22(2), 233-261.

Driving Transversal Collaboration in Ecosystems

Nicolas Bürer

Abstract
The coverage around disruptive events is often overwhelmingly negative. But there is another narrative as well. One in which upheavals act as accelerators of change. By embracing this change and proactively channeling developments, we can break into a bright new future. The article explores three angles to drive transversal ecosystem collaboration: create powerful infrastructure, create space for inspiration, and share knowledge, ideas, and data.

Author
Nicolas Bürer studied Physics at the École polytechnique fédérale de Lausanne (EPFL), Switzerland. After several years in management consulting and young startups, he went on to co-found Movu, of which he still is Chairman. Movu was acquired through a Swiss insurance Group in 2017. Since October 2016, Nicolas Bürer is Managing Director at digitalswitzerland. Nicolas was awarded „Swiss Business Angel of the Year" in 2018. He is a passionate entrepreneur and startup investor.

1 Introduction

I still remember when 2020 was "the future": the date that set the scene for science fiction films; the goal for strategy, innovation and think tanks. Now the new decade is here – and what a time of turbulence and disruption it has been so far. Sociopolitical unrest, a global pandemic and recessionary trends leave little room for cheer in a predominantly gloomy news landscape.

Reporting around disruptive events – is often predominantly negative. But there is another narrative. One where upheaval acts as an accelerator of change. Where the trends we are facing connect us across sociodemographic groups, industries and geographies. And where, if we embrace that change and proactively channel developments, we can emerge into a bright new future.

We are standing at a crossroads. Which path do we take? I believe one leads to a world where effective ecosystems support us all in a hybrid digital future – provided we invest now in transversal collaboration. Transversal means cutting through all sectors of society, politics, business, education and academia. Collaboration means breaking the silos and working together to achieve a much greater result than would be possible alone.

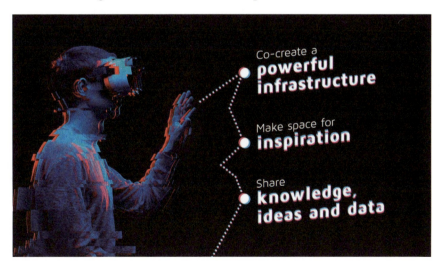

This figure sets out the layers of effective transversal collaboration and the prerequisites for effective ecosystems. In this following, we explore three angles on driving transversal collaboration in ecosystems.

2   Co-create a Powerful Infrastructure

Historically, infrastructure has been a great enabler of change. The development of the steam engine was a major driver in the first industrial revolution. Suddenly, mechanization was possible at scale and goods could be transported by rail. Next came electricity – and the grid – which enabled mass production on assembly lines. Since then, computer-assisted technology and automation – the third phase of industrialization – have paved the way for today's fourth industrial revolution. Early adopters of smart factories are pioneering cyber physical systems that are intelligently linked to each other as well as various stakeholders – suppliers, distributors, marketers, consumers – in complex supply chains. This paradigm shift reflects a more general evolution from industry to ecosystem. But like in the other phases of industrial revolution, digital transformation depends on excellent infrastructure.

Fundamental physical requirements are things like fiber-optic broadband in all cities, fast hotspots in rural areas, secure data centers, access to devices, affordable internet for all sectors of society and reliable electricity supplies to power it all. In some countries, the Government is coordinating a standardized approach by telecommunications companies, electricity providers, cable operators and landlords. This early investment in collaboration is vital if we are to safeguard a future-proof network.

Then there are the non-physical aspects. A robust legal framework for digital activities. Acceptance of digital channels in government administration, political debate, healthcare and commerce. And strategies to ensure data integrity, sovereignty and security. Ethical concerns must not go unanswered; rather, it is vital that companies and politicians engage with all stakeholders to find mutually acceptable solutions. At present, people do not have adequate or easy control over their data. Ideally, we should all be able to save or delete our data decentrally and release selected information as and when we see fit. Now is the time for the public sectors to catch up with banks and build portals for taxes, social security and administrative procedures. A secure digital identity would enable people to simply tap or click for official documents and give them transparency over their administrative data.

We should feel confident that our data is secure and protected from manipulation or theft. Confidence has been eroded in recent years by high-profile data leaks. Who do we trust to establish all important data governance? How can ensure that legislation does not lag behind developments as digital transformation continues? We need to address concerns head-on so that we can get data protection and ethics embedded in law before we face big new questions.

Besides investing today in our digital infrastructure, we need to think ahead. The COVID-19 pandemic of 2020 served as a wake-up call for many that our digital infrastructure is not entirely resilient under pressure. We realized in those months under lockdown how much our working world, cultural life, consumption habits, scientific progress, economic success and democratic debate depend on cables, hardware, software and platforms. And we glimpsed a future where all these facets of life were almost entirely digital. Safeguarding fast data transfer is one thing, but the technology industry will certainly be exploring how to accelerate development of touchless interfaces. Whatever form hardware takes, infrastructure is the vital link between digital and analogue worlds.

The role of knowledge must also not be neglected. If fiber-optic broadband is the railway, and devices and software the trains, then people are the drivers and passengers in the journey to a digital future.

3   Make Space for Inspiration

In our hybrid future, we work, live, love both online and off. We enjoy e-sport and local tournaments; online and widow shopping; House Party and birthday parties; home schooling and forest school; virtual exhibitions and real vernissages. Combining digital and analogue channels offers a rich cultural tapestry for all. So, it comes as no surprise that new digital business models are expanding the channels through which we experience leisure.

Already, you can book spa treatments at home, get 5* meals delivered to your door. You can see zoo animals on webcams and enjoy red alpine skies on Instagram. And this is just the beginning: more digitalization means more machines, robotics, drones and artificial intelligence. But the sensual, innovative, questioning aspects are reserved for us. And that is a good thing. Because experiences engineered by algorithms are neat, predictable – boring even. It is why we need more than ever to invest in the abilities that distinguish us from machines. Yes, they are more efficient than we are, have better memories and exceptional computing power. But the future belongs to our children. And we need bright, structure-free spaces in which to grow our ideas, imagination and empathy.

There is, or course, a role to be played by digital tools and enablers. Just look at how social media has transformed the way people connect and exchange information and ideas over the last fifteen years. But if we are to have an innovative, exciting future, we should also invest in restaurants, museums, botanical gardens, festivals, in literature and theatre. It is when humans meet that we cultivate our senses, in unfamiliar settings and in-person conversations that our thoughts take a new direction. To breathe life into our hybrid future, we have to cultivate both the digital and analogue.

Besides benefiting quality of life, an inspiring environment drives innovation in the start-up scene as well. New ecosystems depend on bold ideas and innovative businesses models. If start-ups are to flourish, we need to help ideas, skills, knowledge and data flow. New ways of thinking are the first step in unusual collaborations that erase industry lines and build new ecosystems. Companies large and small, young and old need to work together and learn from each other to find their place in the future.

If we make space for inspiration, collaboration will follow.

4   Share Knowledge, Ideas, and Data

We know from our experience during the 2020 covid-19 pandemic that schools, the media, museums, libraries and universities can function even in lockdown. While we can be grateful that learning opportunities and knowledge transfer were possible in emergency mode, our task now is to safeguard these important processes for a hybrid future where digital and analogue connections coexist. The various players of our knowledge society need to work together to drive long-term transformation of information repositories, learning and knowledge transfer. That means engaging in dialogue with each other and with other stakeholders, for example in the debate on a single secure digital identity.

The education ecosystem plays a fundamental role in driving transversal collaboration. In a world where much content is relayed electronically – online lectures, podcasts, learning apps, project forums – flexible study is easier and less bureaucratic. Digital learning opens-up a host of new opportunities, allowing individuals to dip into modules beyond their core subject, or complete a guest semester at another institution. As lifelong learning grows in importance, people will be able to return to education more easily and define the pace and schedule to suit their needs. These developments naturally drive transversal collaboration as individual learners take their knowledge, experience and networks with them into society and the economy.

Exchange and knowledge sharing in the scientific community has always been at the heart of advances at the frontiers of knowledge. Digital transformation has already done much to promote a lively and healthy dialogue, in real time, between experts, with government, and before a global audience.

Interdisciplinary working groups are at the forefront of the greatest advances of our age.

Worldwide life sciences industry is a good example of how sectors are transitioning away from a silo structure and towards an ecosystem approach. Big Pharma acts as incubator for smaller R&D setups, while collaboration with academic institutions safeguards a pipeline of talent and ideas. Recently, some jurisdictions have introduced a tax reform program based on patent box and R&D deductions to incentivize innovation. Ensuring attractive framework conditions is one-way governments can contribute to an innovative mindset and culture of collaboration.

When life sciences team up with tech to mine data, the results can be impressive. There are countless examples, but here is one: virtual screening in pharmaceutical research. This approach has taken off in recent years as the volume of data has increased and researchers have been able to access it more easily thanks to user-friendly tools and interfaces. By screening hundreds, thousands, even millions of chemical substances using computational models, R&D departments can identify drug candidates for further development in record time. All this is possible thanks to collaboration between chemists, technology developers, bioinformaticians, statisticians. Accelerating this traditionally laborious and time-consuming phase, financial resources can be invested in driving progress for all.

The pharmaceutical industry is also collaborating with others in the healthcare ecosystem to realize the promise of personalized medicine. As a society, we could support this development by stepping up efforts to digitalize patient data and records. Artificial intelligence is already being used to prescribe medication, recognize patterns in symptoms, analyze medical screening images. But deeper insights from large (anonymized) cohorts are not being exploited enough. And at the individual level, significant time and effort is lost – at the expense of healthcare quality – through a lack of communication between players in different healthcare settings.

The use cases we have explored here hint at the wealth of possible collaborative constellations in a hybrid future. Our task is to support the process through enablers like strong infrastructure, robust data protection and a culture of exchange.

5 Outlook

For many, 2020 is proving something of a turning point. A chance to press pause and reflect on how we want our future to be. A highly disruptive pandemic has coincided with megatrends and challenges like digitalization, demographic change and climate concerns. These are forcing us to define a new pathway not only for society as a whole, but also for each of us individually. The digital new deal needs to integrate these different aspects, but also address social inequalities to ensure existing divides do not widen and newer ones, like digital literacy, do not become divisive.

As we stand at the crossroads to a new normal, collaboration triggers a virtuous circle of inclusion in our hybrid future. By working together now to envision and establish a safe and secure digital infrastructure, we lay the foundations for a successful and satisfying digital economy and society. This is our chance to integrate concerns like climate change and demographic shifts to design a sustainable future.

Section D:
Legal Perspectives on Ecosystem Governance

The Group as a Guiding Model for Ecosystem Governance

Felix Horber and Christina Lusti

Abstract
Business Ecosystems are on the rise. Research is still in the early stages on what the appropriate governance framework for them should be. In this paper, we recognize that a corporation's corporate governance framework and principles can serve as a model for ecosystem governance in many ways. The governance framework should aim to reduce risk, ensure compliance, define roles and responsibilities, and support information flow. The governance principles should support the ecosystem's business success and value creation and ensure that the ecosystem is fit for competition and regulatory challenges.

Authors
Dr. Felix Horber, attorney-at-law, Executive M.B.L.-HSG, has been Group Company Secretary and Managing Director at Swiss Re since 2007. Felix Horber is the author of several books and articles in the field of Swiss corporate law and corporate governance. He is a Lecturer in Law at the University of St. Gallen, Switzerland, and an additional judge at the Superior Court of the Canton of Zug.

Christina Lusti is Head Corporate Governance Group and Director at Swiss Re. Previously, she was Corporate Secretary & Legal Counsel at GAM Holding AG and held several roles with the legal department of Zurich Insurance Group. Christina Lusti is qualified as an attorney-at-law, holding a law degree and an Executive M.B.L. from the University of St. Gallen (HSG).

1 Introduction

Business ecosystems are becoming increasingly important. One of the principal reasons behind the growing significance of ecosystems is digitalization. Rapid changes in technology have underpinned the rise of ecosystems and provided businesses with new opportunities for cooperation and information exchange. New technology changes how companies can serve their customers. The dependence on mobile devices combined with the influence of the internet lead to new opportunities for linking goods and services (Jacobides 2019).

While ecosystems develop very rapidly, not much is known about the governance structures they have. The purpose of this essay is to discuss whether the governance framework of an internationally active group of companies (a publicly listed corporation with multiple subsidiaries, "group") could be a guiding model for the governance of an ecosystem. Furthermore, we evaluate whether it is beneficial for an ecosystem to apply governance principles that have been set out by a group.

The type of ecosystem we refer to in this essay is described by Avramakis et al. (2019, 1 & 2) as follows: "Ecosystems are networks of businesses and consumers (online and offline) that support each other with their respective capabilities to deliver greater economic value than would be possible through autonomous operation (...) Ecosystems offer a one-stop shopping solution for services in one area or several different areas." (Avramakis et al. 2019, 2). We refer to business ecosystems ("ecosystem") in the sense of an orchestrating company ("sponsor") offering products and services provided by several complementors ("partner" or "participant"), which generally cover several fields for customers ("user"). Jacobides (2019, 5) found that "in an increasing number of contexts, the firm is no longer an independent strategic actor. Its success depends on collaboration with other firms in an ecosystem spanning multiple sectors." The value that an ecosystem can create depends on the partners participating in it. Very often, the partners provide their services on a shared platform based on shared principles in order to ensure cross-compatibility between the products and services.

As a first step of this analysis, we explore the different natures of an ecosystem compared with a group. In the second step, we will list the challenges and unique features of an ecosystem. This assessment will assist us in defining what an appropriate governance framework for an ecosystem looks like. We will outline the purpose and the cornerstones of a model governance framework for a group and its corresponding governance principles. Lastly, we will implement the group's governance setup for an ecosystem and analyze where the group's governance principles fit the ecosystem's purpose.

2 Characteristics of an Ecosystem versus a Group

To identify the nature of an ecosystem, we will answer several questions, i.e. what does it take for an ecosystem to be able to take off in the first place? What does it take to avoid losing market share after a successful start and what does it take for an ecosystem to secure a sustainable position after a successful start? Research has identified that three critical stages define the lifecycle of an ecosystem (Reeves et al. 2019). An ecosystem first needs to take the opportunity to obtain a large share of the envisaged market. In order to be successful, it must acquire this share quickly. To acquire a large segment of the market, it needs to simultaneously attract partners, users and more participants, who may offer further products and services to attract more customers. In its early stages, an ecosystem must invest in its growth, its processes and its platform. It must therefore be well provided with capital and defer profitability to a later phase of its development. In order to survive, the ecosystem is forced, in the second stage, to evolve and to face competition. It needs to broaden its scope, growing either by responding to further customer demands or by moving into additional markets. Lastly, in the third stage, a successful and sustainable ecosystem must become a leader in its respective market. It needs to flexibly adapt its strategy to its cycles and developments accordingly. Compared to the evolving and highly dynamic nature of an ecosystem, the group, as we discuss it here, is settled and has become a successful market player. It amends its strategy only if required by market or economic developments.

3 Challenges of an Ecosystem

According to Avramakis et al. (2019), an ecosystem fails if it does not successfully engage partners, offer them attractive incentives or if it underestimates the importance of gaining a critical number of participants that favor profitability. Participants are connected to the ecosystem through the sharing of resources and data. They have governance challenges such as the allocation of resources or dealing with conflicts of interest related to the distribution of costs and gains (Cunningham et al. 2017). As outlined by Avramakis et al. (2019), another important consideration is an ecosystem that fails due to an imbalance between openness and control. The ecosystem must not be too tight nor too open. Jacobides (2019) sees two key governance choices for ecosystems. In the first, the sponsor must decide early on during the creation whether the ecosystem will be open, managed or closed. Depending on the level of openness, the partners can participate in the ecosystem based on general standards, specific rules, or their participation requires approval and is tightly controlled. The more open an ecosystem is, the easier it is to attract partners. There is a tension between having many partners providing services and products and concurrently ensuring high-quality standards as well as profitable value creation for participants. In the second option, the sponsor has the choice between an ecosystem that grants easy access for partners, and one to which partners are tightly bound. The latter yields greater exclusivity of products and services, as well as higher quality standards. A well-known, attractive sponsor and a closed ecosystem will be able to pull in many interested partners. For a smaller sponsor, the number of potential partners attracted depends on the alternatives that partners have. Schmeiss et al. (2019) have identified access, control and incentives as the three overarching governance mechanisms for ecosystems that operate through a platform. Access criteria and rights are defined so as to enable the participation of the relevant partners. Control defines the standards that form the basis for partners to participate, and incentives aim at attracting partners.

4 Group Corporate Governance

How can the described choices be embedded in the governance of an ecosystem? Could the governance framework of a group serve as a guiding model? In line with the described characteristics of a group being solid, well-positioned, profitable and successful, the purpose of its governance is to minimize risks, adhere to regulatory requirements, define authorities and ensure the flow of information. A group governance framework provides organizational structure, oversight and management principles as well as reporting procedures. It clearly allocates roles, responsibilities and authorities, as well as line management reporting within the group. Several documents govern such types of governance framework and its principles. At the uppermost level of hierarchy, a code of conduct or similar document sets out key principles that guide the group's companies in making responsible decisions and achieving results using the highest ethical standards. Articles of Association define the legal and organizational framework of the group parent company. Similarly, corresponding bylaws define the governance framework and include both, the oversight body's responsibilities and those delegated to the management body, including the authorities of their members. Group-wide standards allow steering of the group companies in an efficient and harmonized manner. Such standards may be on topics such as strategy, decisions on group-wide steering and control, allocation of capital and resources to opportunities, asset and liability management, treasury, funding and capital management, finance and risk management, governance, compliance, legal and regulatory affairs, as well as functional issues such as human resources, talent management, reputation and brand. The group's governance principles and standards ensure a consistent, harmonized and tailored governance approach across the group. Its corporate governance complies with local rules and regulations that apply where it does business. Overall, a group's governance framework ensures sustainability, fosters transparency and facilitates a quality assessment of the group's organization and business.

5 Ecosystem Governance

Whether the outlined group governance framework and governance principles could serve as a guiding model for an ecosystem is yet to be evaluated in this essay. If yes, which aspects should an ecosystem consider implementing in its governance? In light of the above considerations on the nature and challenges of an ecosystem, it would seem advisable that the governance of an ecosystem follows the same purpose as that of a group's governance. That is to say, the ecosystem's governance should support reducing risk, ensure compliance with regulatory requirements, define roles and responsibilities and make sure information flows between the sponsor and the partners. According to Colombo et al. (2017), the governance of ecosystems is about governing relationships to achieve competitive advantages, coordinating, motivating and governing the business network. Cunningham et al. (2017) found that an efficient and functioning governance of an ecosystem should ensure that all participants who contribute to the ecosystem's value creation should receive a return on the value that they create together. To this end, and similar to a group, an ecosystem needs to implement not only organizational structure and oversight as well as management controls, but also policies governing the cooperation and participation of the partners. Appropriate documentation relating to the governance framework and governance principles is just as important for an ecosystem as for a group. The documents support the implementation of the ecosystem's governance structure and standards, while fostering understanding among partners of the ecosystem's governance. Taking into account the level of ecosystem openness the sponsor has decided on, the documents ensure a consistent governance approach across the ecosystem. To sum up the above considerations, the governance structure and principles for an ecosystem need to be adapted to the dynamic nature of an ecosystem, as well as to the requirements set by each lifecycle. The governance framework needs to be robust enough to protect the sponsor, yet flexible and adaptable enough to allow the ecosystem to continuously evolve. It is essential that the governance of an ecosystem leaves room for flexibility, so that it may be continuously aligned with the adapted strategy. An attractive governance framework supports the sponsor in attracting partners. An open culture also plays an important role. Sponsor and partner culture and governance should fit well with each other.

6 Conclusions

Good governance is very much in the interests of stakeholders, which include investors, shareholders, clients and employees. In general, corporate governance continues to progress towards increased transparency and accountability of companies to stakeholders. The same demands apply for ecosystems. One example being the concerns which have been raised lately with regards to competition and data protection law issues related to ecosystems. Corresponding laws and the understanding of what should be permissible vary a lot from one country to another. A meaningful and comprehensive dialogue with stakeholders, including regulators, is important, not only for large groups but also for large ecosystems. This being said, appropriate governance frameworks for ecosystems may vary considerably from one to the next, according to the specific setups and choices of each individual ecosystem. One governance structure might be suitable for one ecosystem but not for another. It is however safe to recognize that, for all types of ecosystems, the governance framework and principles must support business opportunities and value creation, while ensuring the desired level of standards and controls in order to remain competitive and face regulatory challenges.

Literature

Avramakis, E., Anchen, J., & Raverkar, A.K. (2019). Digital ecosystems: extending the boundaries of value creation in insurance. Swiss Re Institute, 1-5.

Colombo, M.G., Dagnino, G.B., Lehmann, E.E., & Salmador, M.P. (2017). The governance of entrepreneurial ecosystems. Small Business Economics, 419-428.

Cunningham, J.A., Menter, M., & Wirsching, K. (2017). Entrepreneurial ecosystem governance: a principal investigator-centered governance framework. Small Business Economics, 545-562.

Jacobides, M.G. (2019). In the ecosystem economy, what's your strategy? Harvard Business Review, 97(5), 128-137.

Reeves, M., Lotan, H., Legrand, J., & Jacobides, M.G. (2019). How business ecosystems rise (and often fall). MIT Sloan Management Review, 60(4), 1-6.

Schmeiss, J., Hoelzle, K., & Tech, R.P.G. (2019). Designing governance mechanisms in platform ecosystems: Addressing the paradox of openness through blockchain technology. California Management Review, Vol. 62(1), 121-143.

The Association as a Guiding Model for Ecosystem Governance

Dante Alighieri Disparte

Abstract
As organizations explore new ways to structure their collaboration models, Diem, which is committed to building a payments network, chose the association as the legal structure to bring together all parties that have chosen to participate in the initiative. The article explains Diem's initial rationale for choosing this particular legal structure to drive collaboration in an ecosystem, taking into account the different interests of the parties involved as well as regulatory requirements.

Author
Dante Alighieri Disparte is Chief Strategy Officer and Head of Global Policy at Circle and former Vice Chairman and Head of Policy and Communications at the Diem Association. He is also a member of the Federal Emergency Management Agency's National Advisory Council and Founder and Chairman of Risk Cooperative. He serves on the World Economic Forum's Digital Currency Governance Consortium.

When it comes to technology efforts, especially those with open-source principles, new standards of governance are called upon. This is true when the code base is released to the world to spur the development of digital commons and to benefit from the collective assurance of thousands of eyes. These types of efforts require the suspension of not only disbelief, but in many cases the suspension of long held norms driving the governance of traditional efforts and enterprises.

In many respects, while the technology underpinning ecosystems clearly produces breakthroughs and facilitates market adoption, growth and innovation, the real breakthrough especially in heavily regulated sectors, comes from organizing principles, for which governance is the key. All other matters being equal, governance has proven time and again to be the real difference maker. Core components that drive the governance of the Diem Association and the mission of creating financial infrastructure that supports the twin goals of financial inclusion and responsible financial services innovation to pull billions of people into the perimeter of payments, is a pari passu governance principle.

In this organizing concept, members of the Association follow a voting and operating model based on equal weighting. In short, one member, one vote. In addition to this approach, key organizational decisions flow through an inverted pyramid of decision making and consensus.

Where traditionally large organizations are governed by narrow bodies – e.g. the board of directors of most publicly held companies comprise fewer than nine people making the most consequential decisions. Over time, as the Association grows its membership, the most consequential votes will be presented to the council requiring either a majority or supermajority voting model.

As an additional guardrail, the concept of public license enshrined in regulatory approval and alignment, is the pursuit of a path of technological innovation based on permission rather than forgiveness. In short, seeking regulatory oversight on a same risk, same rules basis as peer operators ensures that public interests are of paramount importance. Going one line further, Swiss financial regulations introduce the concept of regulatory locks, which take certain promises, operating norms and other standards as an additional precondition for ongoing license to operate.

Naturally, like other complex organizing principles, governance evolves over time and varies in conditions of stress or potential ambiguity. Herein, the ability to fully describe the spectrum of governance, organizing principles, authorities and powers along an axis of normal operating conditions, through to periods of stress is essential. As an ecosystem, especially one that envisages broad global participation, it is essential to espouse harmonization, expectations on market conduct and high-assurance pathways instilling trust and confidence in the system overall and its participants. The best way this is achieved, especially with open-source technologies, is the meaningful empowerment and contributions from a broad base of participants.

Unlike traditional siloed operations, technologies or governance models, which are often plagued by single source of failure designs, open-source principles encourage improvements from the broadest base of market participants, irrespective of their origin. In short, there is (and should not be) any pride of authorship. Rather, pride and power are derived from collective contribution over time. Examples of this approach in the Libra project, include the fact that the code base has been open source since the initial white paper was released on June 18, 2019.

Similarly, the use of so called "bug bounties" to promote the identification and remediation of potential vulnerabilities in code have been implemented from the earliest days of the project. From a cybersecurity perspective, this approach benefits from the collective expertise of a far-reaching base of actors, rather than singularly internalizing operational resilience based on individual (often limited) resources. Indeed, one of the major benefits of blockchain-based systems at the technological, operational and governance levels is the concept of collective witness and collective defense. Where much of the infrastructure that underpins the global financial system is siloed and often concentrated into single points of failure, blockchain structures by virtue of their decentralized nature do not labor under these challenges. Examples include frequent population scale data breaches, or risk management immaturity when it comes to redundancy of traditional systems. In these cases, the failure of governance and the persistence of risks emerging between the proverbial keyboard and the chair are as big a threat to systems, as advanced technological or operational risks.

If governance is the real breakthrough, the greatest manifestation that governance is working, especially with open source or heavily regulated efforts is the degree to which they spur public-private collaboration. After all, especially when it comes to innovation in the financial services domain, the challenges and opportunities are far too great for any one sector (or country for that matter) to go it alone. Today, more than 80 % of the world's central banks are contemplating some form of currency and payment system innovation. This is done in the spirit of supporting broadly shared goals, including financial inclusion, financial stability and protecting and preserving the rules-based financial system.

While technology alone is not a panacea for any of these challenges (or opportunities), the absence of reliable, high-trust digital commons is clearly an area of vulnerability. While much of the discourse of how to appropriately develop and regulate technological innovation at population scale has focused on the risks if these emerging systems prevail. Not nearly enough discourse has been devoted to questions about the absence of trusted digital systems spanning a range of areas – from identity to authentication and basic financial access, ownership and title.

In short, so much of the world's existing, largely analog infrastructure has reached a point of diminishing returns. As a consequence, we need better plans, structures, investment and governance models for modernizing our collective commons on which commerce relies. Extending the perimeter of the formal economy presupposes the existence of digital commons that are at once empowering, compliant and high-assurance, when it comes to operational readiness and security. Afterall, it would be a grave governance error to run a science experiment on something as sacrosanct as people's identity, their hard-earned money and their entrepreneurial endeavors. The final area thus, in the governance of ecosystems stems from fostering market environments that follow a series of first principles.

These first principles include concepts that promote competition, protect consumers, improve optionality and choice and, perhaps most of all, promote free markets and market-based innovations. The blend of apprehension and fear with which many novel technologies and breakthrough innovations are met, especially in highly regulated areas, says as much about the state of play of innovation in certain sectors, as much as it does the state of public oversight that promotes even-handed, technologically neutral approaches to promoting market development.

As the global economy shifts from principles of production that were initially location-based -anchored to the development of physical manufactured goods – to a technology powered, always on model, it is notable that we are relegated to a financial system with "banking hours" operating 9-5, taking weekends off and enjoying almost a dozen bank holidays per year. The case for market-driven innovation is as much a function of harnessing entrepreneurial energy as it is a function of filling a large void in the market. Where past waves of creative destructive market development produced clear winners and losers auguring the world of industrial Robber Barons and tech titans along the way, there is a current trend afoot (albeit small) that realizes a "winner takes all" development model may be at the end of its life.

In its place, especially when it relates to ecosystems, decentralized structures and infrastructure more generally, must attract collective investment in order to maintain value for participants, contributors and beneficiaries alike. In this spirit, some ecosystems spark the concept of cooperative competition (or coopetition) when it comes to building collective commons on which trade, market access or business model transformation relies. Examples include collective investments in wireless infrastructure, investments in both the hardware and software that powers the internet – including a vast global array of subsea cables – and other forms of public-private infrastructure.

This requirement of long-term investment in order to promote viability, combat obsolescence and respond to market demands or forces too great for one player to address on their own, necessitates that economically viable business models can be supported by an ecosystem. In this way, with the internet, road systems, public and private utilities, among others, are the best examples of how ecosystems should be governed with a long-term view in mind. This breaks the traditional short-term profit maximizing investment model, which often produces corner cutting decision making. In its place, investors in ecosystems favor longevity, viability and a veritable all ships rising proposition. Industry bodies, like those international governance bodies that help drive entire sectors, from airlines to the internet and wireless standards, among others, all espouse governance models that help build trust and confidence, while harmonizing operating standards for ecosystem participants.

The same must hold true as the prospect of open-source ecosystems entering finance and other regulated markets appears imminent. In the same way platforms of developers building applications in various app stores building value – in a "whole is greater than the sum of the parts model" – opportunities to spur responsible (and broad) financial services innovation is similarly compelling over the long run. Unlocking the real potential of fintech innovation requires equilibrium between the goals of innovation, inclusion and compliance, which for far too long have been seen as competing objectives, rather than coequal goals. The challenges open, financial ecosystems aim to address are simply far too great for any one actor to address on their own. In this spirit, the twin goals of financial inclusion and responsible financial services innovation are invigorated by the UN Sustainable Development Goals (SDGs).

The SDGs call for the reduction of remittance costs, as one example, from the stubbornly high global average of 7% to 3% by 2030 in order to put more hard-earned money back into the hands of their intended beneficiaries. Short of open digital transformation of the financial system and the inclusion of more than 1.7 billion people who are outside of the formal economy as unbanked people, there are few viable, good ideas to address this challenge at scale.

Herein lies the central organizing question for the creation of uncommon coalitions – what can we do together, that we cannot do on our own? Building ecosystems, digital commons and spurring long term innovation, investments and solutions is the only way to meaningfully address some of the world's most deleterious challenges. Whether we are addressing the increasingly chaotic effects of climate change, or insidious rates of financial exclusion and sociopolitical polarization, making commerce and economic progress more participatory is essential.

As a final consideration, the dependency of certain sectors, such as banking, nationally important manufacturing and utilities as examples, on an implied public backstop suggests the need for governance models that take this reality into account. While the privatization of gain and socialization of losses was most evident (with the benefit of hindsight) in the aftermath of the 2008 financial crisis, the pattern remains in place across a range of sectors and the ecosystems they are a part of. In responding to the COVID-19 pandemic, as another example, the world has offset trillions of dollars of taxpayer underwritten funds to spur a veritable vaccine development space race (operational Warp Speed in the U.S.).

This is perhaps the largest scale decentralized ecosystem effort to work on a common cause, which is to break the chain of transmission of COVID-19 and help the global economy return to some semblance of normalcy. In this effort, as with past post-crisis eras, values-driven governance that enhances trust, along with mission-aligned ecosystems spurs open collaboration creating new institutions or modernizing existing ones. The one difference is how the use of technologies such as blockchain, enshrine the operation of consortia and governance on equal footing, common cause and collective defense in technological code, as much as organizational conduct. There is no doubt the operating model of technology-powered ecosystems is here to stay. This too is a competitive reality, where the most enduring organizing principle and source of long-term competitive advantage is the trust, reliability and outcomes people derive from contributing to these networks and being on the receiving end of the goods, services and solutions they help power. As the age-old proverb asserts, if you want to go fast, go alone, if you want to go far go together.

Section E: Applications of Ecosystem Governance

Leveraging Digital Ecosystems – How to Transform a Traditional Publisher into a Leading Ecosystem Player

Stefano Santinelli

Abstract

Swisscom Directories (SD) delivered the telephone directory to all Swiss households. With the acquisition of the Yellow Pages, SD also became a publisher, selling advertising to Swiss small and medium-sized enterprises (SMEs). In the early 2000s, however, global technology platforms – such as Google, Amazon, TripAdvisor, Facebook – radically changed the way people search, interact, get information, and shop for products and services. It was clear that SD needed to change, too, to stay relevant. This article describes how SD transformed its entire business to become the leading digital agency for SMEs in Switzerland, thriving in a new, open, digital ecosystem.

Author

Stefano Santinelli has been Chief Executive Officer of Swisscom Directories AG since 2016. He held leading positions at UBS, ABB, SAP, and Microsoft. As an entrepreneur, he was co-founder of skyva and tutti.ch, the leading marketplace for online classifieds in Switzerland. He serves on multiple boards and holds a degree in computer science from the ETH Zurich and an MBA from Rochester Business School.

1 Introduction

Swisscom Directories (SD) was founded at the beginning of the 20th century as an internal department of PTT (the Swiss public communications provider) to create the "good old" telephone directory to be sent to every home in the country. By law, all Swiss telephone numbers had to be listed. Over time, SD became an independent company with the sole purpose of producing and distributing a printed directory of Swiss telephone numbers to every home in Switzerland. With the acquisition of the Yellow Pages, SD became a publisher based on a simple business model: Selling advertising to Swiss small and medium-sized businesses (SMBs) to list their phone number in the directory.

In the early 2000s, however, the world really began to change, in the sense that a single company was no longer an independent strategic player, but that its success depended on collaboration with other companies in an ecosystem. True ecosystems began to emerge, driven by factors such as a convergence of regulatory changes, a blurring of the distinction between products and services, and the increasing use of the Internet (Jacobides 2019). As technology changed the way people interacted, informed themselves, and shopped for products and services, it was clear that SD also needed to change to stay in business. In 2004, SD moved its printed telephone directory to the Internet and launched the online directory local.ch. The business model did not change until 2015, when SD realigned the entire business to become the leading digital agency for Swiss SMEs.

Rising digital ecosystems forced SD to a radical transformation. This happened in three cycles (a publisher of a phone book until 2004, a provider of online directories from 2004 to 2015 and a digital agency from 2015) and ended with SD achieving record profits by 2019.

This is a brief overview of how SD has done just that; how it has learned to embrace the ecosystem, play a role in it, and how it has thrived as a result.

2 The Disruptive Force of Digitalization

Three major paradigm shifts have disrupted the SD business model and caused SD to realign its traditional core business.
1. The rise of free services threatens the SD business model
2. Technological breakthroughs that drastically change user behavior
3. The rise of advertising technology disrupting the advertising market

The first paradigm shift for SD was the arrival of free services enabled by the rise of global platforms (notably Google, Facebook, Amazon, Tripadvisor, and Apple). Starting in 2000, a plethora of products were given away. People could search for free, download videos for free, connect with professional colleagues on LinkedIn and friends on Facebook – all for free. "For the Google generation, the Internet is the land of the free," as Chris Anderson of the Wall Street Journal said (2009). The minority of customers who pay subsidize the majority who do not. In many cases, a few advertisers pay for content so that many consumers can get it cheaply or for free. This technological revolution put the reach and engagement of SD's own products into much more perspective, as customers now had access to global platforms with billions of users and hours of daily engagement. For free.

Take the search. In the analog past, if you wanted to find a plumber in Switzerland, you might look at ads in the local newspaper or flip through the Yellow Pages. In the early 2000s, search engines quickly became the first port of call for any search – for information, for products, for services. According to a report by the University of Zurich on Swiss Internet usage, the majority of Swiss internet users (87%) search the Internet for product information (Latzer, Büchi, and Festic 2019).

Technology also influenced the way people communicate and consume information. People turned to social networks to share news and information and connect easily. According to Online Karma, 71% of Swiss people use social media in Switzerland. 3.4 million Swiss people use Facebook alone, (out of a population of 8.5 million). Companies have realized that they can use these platforms to engage customers. Take LinkedIn, the professional social media site with 2.9 million active users in Switzerland: SMBs can publish a profile and use this platform to acquire new customers. For free.

At the same time, instant messaging on platforms like Messenger and WhatsApp was being used by consumers who wanted to communicate quickly and in closed groups. Companies realized they could use the same technologies to connect with consumers and solve problems, but also to market to them. In Switzerland, the use of instant messaging services like WhatsApp has more than doubled since 2011. In 2019, 91% of Swiss people used such services. (Latzer, Büchi, and Festic 2019).

The second paradigm shift was technological breakthroughs. The very high penetration of cell phone use worldwide and in Switzerland created an environment where almost everyone had instant access to all the free services described above. Deloitte's Global Mobile Consumer Survey of over 1,000 consumers found that 92% of all adults in Switzerland own a smartphone, of which 97 % use their device daily. (Grampp and Brandes 2019). In this brave new world dominated by GAFA (Google, Amazon, Facebook, Apple), technological breakthroughs changed the way we use services as user-friendly technologies began to spill over from the consumer tech world to the business world. Amazon's Alexa smart speaker could be used to find products or services ("Alexa, find me a hairdresser in Zurich"). The app economy took off, and an iPhone or Android app could instantly connect you to all sorts of services. According to app analytics firm App Annie (Perez 2017), the global app economy will be worth $6.3 trillion by 2021, up from $1.3 trillion last year.

And technology didn't just bring potential customers to informative websites – customers increasingly shopped online. In Switzerland, 82 % of consumers said they buy things online and 76 % compare prices of products or services online (Latzer, Büchi, and Festic 2019).

The third paradigm shift was a drastic change in the advertising market with the development of advertising technology.

The evolution of advertising technologies has not only improved efficiency and transparency, but also fundamentally changed the way to select, target and reach customers. Traditionally, an advertiser selected the website and the placement of an ad using the website as a proxy for the target audience, i.e., if a marketer wanted to target men aged 35 and over with an income of $150,000, they would place an ad on a website like Forbes.com. The evolution of ad tech means that the advertiser could have tools which actively look for the desired target audience on large global plattforms (GAFA) powered by artificial intelligence (Dempster and Lee 2015).

In summary, users no longer needed to use SD directories to search for businesses, but instead relied on cell phones, search engines, and social media to find everyday services. On the other hand, SMBs were able to advertise for free on these platforms and gain access to millions of users every day. Furthermore, SMBs no longer wanted simple advertising in static directories, but wanted to hunt for customers online via personalized messaging." As a result, SD's online directories local.ch and search.ch – very popular until 2012 and the core of the SD business model – started to decline and become irrelevant. SMB customers started to churn, switching to free offers. SD's traditional and proven business model was being disrupted by new digital ecosystems.

It was clear that SD had to play a new role in a radically changed universe. It was also clear that SD had to help its customers – 300,000 SMEs in Switzerland – meet the challenge of marketing themselves in this brave new world. Typically, a hairdresser in Aarau who used to advertise in the phone book does not have the strategic marketing knowledge or digital intelligence to develop his own online marketing strategy and take advantage of the emerging global online platforms.

3 Towards an Ecosystem Model

SD had to change as a company to move from being a phone book company and local search player within a clear, fixed ecosystem where it owned the channels, to playing a role in an open, free, cross-channel and technology-enabled ecosystem. It was about redefining the purpose of the company while staying true to its roots – supporting Swiss SMEs. SD reformed its business to focus on driving SMB success in the digital world: on owned platforms, in the GAFA ecosystem and in technology-enabled business models. In short, it became the marketing partner of choice for SMBs in the digital world.

First, SD reviewed its operations and philosophy using the ecosystem approach – and indeed overhauled itself to be more like some of the tech players in the new ecosystem. Its credo was "fast and open innovation."

Exhibit 1: The transition from the old to the new world

– The speed and agility of the business had to change. SD used to have a slow and rigid product development/planning cycle of over 3 years and 1 product per year. Instead, it moved to a quarterly innovation cycle better aligned with the pace of technology innovation so customers could benefit from the latest products. This was reflected in a flatter management structure with only 3 levels instead of 5 and the introduction of OKRs (Objectives

and Key Results), a framework attributed to Andy Grove, CEO of Intel, who introduced the approach there and defined that the key result must be measurable (Doerr 2018). The company moved to having quarterly rather than annual key performance indicators.
- SD has evolved from focusing exclusively on its core business and building its own products/proprietary developments to a portfolio of big bets that leverages an ecosystem to deliver scalable solutions.
- SD has changed its view of the property. For example, data, how to get it, use it, manage it. Before, they were "owned" by SDs in directories (data is verified, authenticated, 100 % accurate). The company had to philosophically change its mindset to a marketplace view where data is crowdsourced, and instead of it having to be accurate, it's "good enough." SD used to "own" the entire sales process and all customers and users – it switched to being part of an omni-channel ecosystem where it shares processes, products and customers.
- In summary, SD has evolved from a specialized market maker in "directories", i.e., a publisher, to a company operating in cooperation in an open global ecosystem, i.e., a marketing agency.

Second, SD reviewed its product portfolio by applying the same ecosystem credo and asking the questions of how disruptive it will be to the market and how close/far it will be from SD's business – and only then decided how it would create the product. Did SD need to develop the product or service itself? Or did it make more sense to use existing international service providers? Did it make sense to partner with them? Or did SD need to acquire and integrate their products or even start a new company to meet the need?

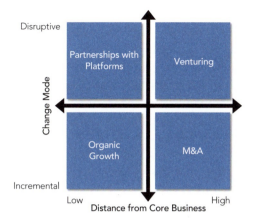

Exhibit 2: Innovation mode selection

- If the product involves only incremental change in the market and is close to SD's core business, the product would be developed within the company. An example of this would be SD's own vertical market comparison sites. SD launched 55 platforms that compare local service providers.
- When the product brings only incremental change to the market and has a large distance to SD's core business, SD decided to acquire and integrate it. For example, the company offers SMEs a marketing tool (customer relationship management software), a booking platform and a direct marketing tool, called MyCockpit, as a software as a service offering. To do this, it acquired the Swiss operations of Shore (a German CRM company) and integrated them into the company. The same was true for Localina, an Internet-based restaurant reservation system that SD acquired from a Portuguese start-up.
- If the product brought high disruptive change to the market, but was still close to SD's core business, SD partnered with global platforms. For example, SD offers a service, digitalONE, where it manages the SMB profile on third-party platforms on their behalf and ensures that corporate information is always consistent and up-to-date on more than 25 online services. To achieve this, SD partnered with a global player, Yext, which has developed a data management tool to manage a company's location-based information on multiple directories. SD did the same with MyCommerce, where it manages the sales channels of our SMEs on platforms such as Amazon, Instagram, ebay, Google Shopping on their behalf. To do this, SD partnered with Ecwid, a tool for small business owners to easily set up an online store.

- If the product represented a high disruptive change for the market but was far from SD's core business, SD looked into creating a new company. For example, Adunit AG was formed by SD to focus on programmatic advertising (the automated buying and selling of online advertising) sold to SMB customers as our MyCampaign product. However, SD realized that owning a software business was not its core competency: it is difficult to develop a software business in a local market like Switzerland that can compete with global offerings. Instead, SD decided to resell an existing global platform called iPromote. The lesson learned was that the Swiss market did not have enough volume to compete with global platforms. So in this case, SD pivoted to the ecosystem.

4 The Outcome

The shift to an ecosystem-based business showed clear results. First, product cycles have really accelerated. Instead of one product in seven years, SD has switched to seven products in one year. The focus on new products has paid off, with 80 % of the 2019 order intake coming from products that did not exist in 2015. SD now has the most complete offering in the market (presence management, website development, online campaigns, eCommerce, booking and CRM, and cash management). SD fully compensated for declining revenues from old products (such as the printed phone book) with new revenues from online advertising (such as online campaigns on google and Facebook). This did not come at the expense of profits, which grew 15 % between 2015 and 2019. By comparison, some of our competitors (Eniro in Sweden, Yell in the UK, France's Solocal, and Italiaonline in Italy) have seen revenues fall by 30-60 % and are far less profitable. But perhaps on a more existential level, the key to success is that SD has successfully fundamentally changed its operations and strategy to serve its target customers. By leveraging the power of the ecosystem, SD has evolved from a publisher of phone books to the largest digital agency for Swiss SMEs.

Literature

Anderson, C. (2009). The economics of giving it away. Wall Street Journal: January 31.

Dempster, C., & Lee, J. (2015). The rise of the platform marketer: Performance marketing with Google, Facebook, and Twitter, plus the latest high-growth digital advertising platforms. John Wiley & Sons, New York.

Doerr, J. (2018). Measure what matters: How Google, Bono, and the Gates Foundation rock the world with OKRs. Penguin, New York.

Jacobides, M. G. (2019). In the ecosystem economy, what's your strategy? Harvard Business Review. 97(5), 128-137.

Grampp, M. & Brandes, D. (2018). Global mobile consumer survey. Deloitte Report.

Latzer, M., Büchi, M., & Festic, N. (2019). Internet applications and their use in Switzerland. University of Zurich Research Report.

Perez, S. (2017). App economy to grow to $6.3 trillion in 2021, user base to nearly double to 6.3 billion. Tech Crunch: June 27.

The Role of Governance to Grow Ecosystems – Lessons Learned from a Public-private Distributed Ledger Technology Journey

Ulrich Schimpel

Abstract
This article reflects on the development of the Drakkensberg initiative, a public-private multi-party ecosystem to accelerate the end-to-end process for the creation of Swiss companies. A particular focus is on the role of governance in this multilateral context, where all – quite different – partners act at eye level and where the application of a distributed ledger technology (DLT) is not only the enabler for this holistic ecosystem, but also an innovation element entering a long established (manual) process.

Author
Dr. Ulrich Schimpel is Chief Innovation Officer at IBM Switzerland and member of the Corporate Technical Strategy Team. He has over 15 years of industry experience and a special focus on innovative technologies such as AI, blockchain and IoT. He holds a PhD in IT and an EMBA.

1 Introduction

The Drakkensberg ecosystem aims to accelerate the end-to-end process of establishing a standard Swiss company from several weeks to as few days as possible – or even 48 hours. The partners of this multi-leader DLT ecosystem are two commercial register offices, a bank, several notaries and law firms, and three IT companies. They all operate at eye level without a hierarchy or dedicated ecosystem leader.

The idea was born in a technology venture competition in April 2017 and a successful demo followed in April 2018, when the entire process to create and register Drakkensberg AG was completed in less than two hours. The minimally viable ecosystem officially launched in January 2019 and by April 2020, more than 60 companies had been founded through the Drakkensberg ecosystem – with plans to expand to more partners.

During the journey of the Drakkensberg ecosystem, the challenges manifested in:
- Easy and agile control of all partners at eye level
- Ecosystem innovation in parallel with the introduction of a new technology
- Gradual development of the ecosystem with partners and activities at different speeds.

Governance plays an essential role in all these challenges. We will take a closer look at some key aspects, their interrelationships and the insights we have gained on our joint journey.

2 DLT Ecosystems and Innovation

Few technologies are, by definition, as closely associated with business ecosystems as distributed ledger technology (DLT), with blockchain arguably its most prominent representative. DLTs are still a fairly new phenomenon across all industries, which basically makes every DLT project a joint innovation journey of the business ecosystem involved and its associated partners.

As innovations and ecosystems are complex topics in themselves, the successful realization and commercialization of a combination of both proves to be extremely challenging in practice.

Lessons learned:
Already during the first ideation workshop with all partners in 2017, it became clear that individual parties had little or no understanding of the domain of the other parties. The existing manual process had masked these gaps, which now had to be uncovered and eliminated together if a true end-to-end (digital) process was to be realized. One of the first challenges was to create an open environment with a common perspective, language and mechanism for collaboration. In our case, it proved extremely helpful to leverage the neutral terrain and (implicit) governance of a Swiss supra-organizational technology venture competition, where all partners were respected and interacted as equals.

3 Joint Value Proposition and Coordination

The joint value proposition is the starting point for all necessary activities and actors – explicitly including those outside the control of ecosystem leaders (Adner 2017, 44) – and defines the "(endogenous) boundary of the relevant ecosystem" (Adner 2017, 43).

Most ecosystems agree on an ecosystem leader, which simplifies many aspects of coordination and defining a joint value proposition. In our case, a single leader was not accepted by the participants and posed significant challenges to the joint value proposition of the Drakkensberg ecosystem: How to take into account the very different perspectives of the various parties? How to condense them into a compelling and competitive articulation of the value proposition? How to find a joint governance approach – as opposed to extended governance driven by a single ecosystem leader – to enable effective coordination?

Lessons learned:
The application of modern problem-solving and innovation techniques such as design thinking enabled participants to develop the joint value proposition of "reducing the time to start a standard Swiss company from several weeks to a few days". This fits well with Switzerland's image of being a leading innovation location. The estimated 20,000 standard company start-ups per year showed a sufficient market potential for some of the workshop participants to embark on this ecosystem journey. All partners agreed to use their resources to the best of their ability while maintaining their traditional business model, i.e. notary, bank and commercial register each independently charge their original fees.

Coordination and low cost were facilitated by the use of existing standards, (sub)processes and infrastructures and can be seen as one of the key success criteria. Additional digitization and DLT were only introduced where added value was created, e.g., by closing gaps in terms of multilateralism of the ecosystem.

In other words, an implicit joint governance and business model among all partners has been used. This approach has its strength in moving quickly but postpones important issues that need to be addressed at the latest when the ecosystem is to scale from a pilot project to a professional services network. In fact, a dedicated governance and business model workshop was requested and conducted in early 2020 under the facilitation of a highly experienced subject matter expert. This showed that (implicit) guiding principles and a common value proposition are indeed shared by all partners. Nevertheless, there are different opinions about ecosystem priorities and how to achieve the joint value proposition. Without a committed ecosystem leader – a role that also comes with (financial) commitments – no quick decision could be made. The workshop was nevertheless very valuable, as it led to the explicit formulation of the guiding ecosystem principles and the decision to develop a memorandum of understanding that clarifies roles and processes and that can be shared with (potential) new ecosystem partners.

Even after discussions with various experts, there do not seem to be any "simple and efficient recipes" for multi-leader ecosystem coordination today – obviously a topic worth exploring further.

4 Relevant Types of Innovations for DLT Ecosystems

Innovation and co-innovation are closely associated with ecosystems in contemporary research (Bogers, Sims, and West 2019) and business practice – often with a focus on creating or defending a competitive advantage in competitive environments. In the context of DLT ecosystems, two potentially intertwined aspects of innovation come into play, namely "process innovation" and "business model innovation," (e.g., Gassmann, Frankenberger, and Csik 2017), which are linked to the What?, How?, Who?, and Why? of a business model:

- **Process innovation:** DLT offers a distributed approach to interacting at eye level within an (existing) ecosystem – without a clear hierarchy or a single trusted party. Companies are often not used to working in such peer networks. Here, the fundamental challenge is to successfully leverage DLT for more efficient operations (How?) without significantly changing the products (What?), customers (Who?), or business model (Why?).

- **Business model innovation:** This refers to creating a completely new (joint) value proposition for the ecosystem based on truly multilateral relationships. In addition to the challenges of process innovation induced by the DLT "peer network", the aspects of elaborating and leveraging multilateral transactions come into play. Combined, they fundamentally change the entire ecosystem business model – basically all four dimensions (What?, How?, Who?, and Why?). This is probably a key reason why business model innovation in the DLT area is currently still left to startup scenes like CryptoValley in Switzerland.
- **Product innovation:** This refers to the What? In the context of DLT, however, there is no isolated consideration of this dimension, since the use of DLT technology in today's business world is always fundamentally linked simultaneously with an adaptation of processes (How?).

The start of the DLT ecosystem is usually a sensitive, agile journey – especially when it is launched in an existing domain or industry. A delicate balance needs to be struck to keep initial costs within a tolerable range until the revenue curve rises – while providing sufficient incentives for (new) partners to join the ecosystem. The initial growth phase of a DLT ecosystem until it reaches a relevant size can be long – sometimes even years. The development of a typical DLT ecosystem and its relationship to different types of innovations is shown in the following figure.

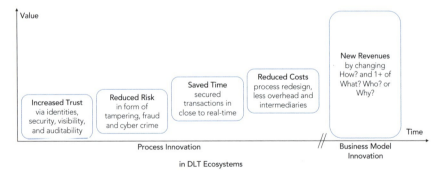

Exhibit 1: Process innovation vs. business model innovation in DLT ecosystems (Schimpel 2019).

Lessons learned:

The Drakkensberg ecosystem predominantly took a "process innovation" approach by digitizing and integrating existing processes without significant changes to the What?, Who? and Why? Looking back at the given context, this seems to be the (most) feasible approach. Many imponderables, a heterogeneous group of partners and legal constraints in each of the areas (banks, notaries and commercial registers) and their interrelationships made it very difficult to realize more than (just) a process innovation. More specifically, the Drakkensberg ecosystem …

- uses process innovation to expose existing partners to the dynamics of DLT solely in its role as technology.
- breaks down the journey into incremental extensions of the ecosystem – aligned with the benefits that come from better visibility and reduced risk – and targets the added value that comes from time and cost reductions.
- plans to work out a business model innovation only after partners are familiar with DLT as a technology and its impact on (ecosystem) processes.
- carefully balances initial costs, additional revenue, and attracting new partners – because it can take a long time to move the DLT ecosystem to the next phase.
- is aware of the diverse competition, coordination issues, and policy concerns through its diverse partners – but lacks an overarching (explicit) ecosystem governance approach.
- reuses existing infrastructures wherever possible and integrates new partners and technologies via standardized and lightweight interfaces.

This approach was widely disputed among the various partners. One group of partners clearly favored a business innovation concept with a completely new business model, a comprehensive business plan and the involvement of (external) investors.

This was one of the moments when the multilateral eye-to-eye approach showed its limitations: no single partner was willing to take the lead and bear the considerable effort to create a complete business innovation concept. In other words: While each partner sees the joint value proposition of the Drakkensberg ecosystem as attractive to itself, no partner expects a sufficiently high return-on-investment to take the overall lead and to invest in the elaboration of a holistic new business model. This is probably exactly why a multilateral "eye-to-eye" ecosystem formed in the first place. In a situation where one party profits strongly, an ecosystem is expected to form around that (natural) leader and their (sufficiently attractive) business model – or no ecosystem forms at all.

So far, the Drakkensberg ecosystem is growing successfully – at a gradual pace – with more than 60 registered companies and concrete actions to scale. However, it remains to be seen if and how truly multilateral (DLT) ecosystems can dynamically and sustainably evolve and create a competitive advantage. It is clear that a more sophisticated, yet lightweight governance model is needed to facilitate further scaling of the Drakkensberg ecosystem.

5 Relevant Risks of Ecosystem Innovation

Risk mitigation is a core element of governance and part of the goal of "keeping it controlled" (Hilb 2016, 117). In a digital environment, additional governance elements are needed to ensure consistent "digital value creation" (Hilb 2018, 15-16). However, most governance models refer to individual organizations. The question arises whether these models are also valid in the context of an (innovation) ecosystem – for individual organizations or even the entire ecosystem.

The traditional innovation only has to convince the consumer, as it does not significantly affect the routines of other partners. Adner (2013, 32) calls this the execution risk, and basically all successful companies have learned to master it effectively.

However, innovation in an increasingly networked business world often requires partners and their routines to change. Two new dimensions come into play here, namely co-innovation risk and adoption chain risk. They "lurk in the blind spot of traditional strategy" and "trying to break out of the mold of incremental innovation is likely to create challenges for the ecosystem" (Adner 2013, 35).

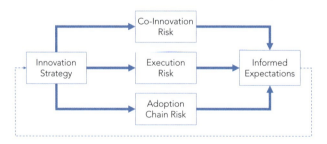

Exhibit 2: The three risks of innovation (Adner 2013, 34)

Execution risk is defined as the "challenges you face in implementing your innovation to the required specifications and within the required time." (Adner 2013, 33). Individual execution risk is not the focus of this paper because the "traditional tools of strategy, marketing, operations, and project management provide excellent guidance for identifying and managing execution risk" (Adner 2013, 34).

Co-innovation risk is defined as the "extent to which the successful commercialization of your innovation depends on the successful commercialization of other innovations" (Adner 2013, 33).

Part of co-innovation risk is ensuring that all partners are motivated and capable of innovating together with your company. Even if this is given, there is still a probability that each individual innovation will not be successful – just like your own innovation, see execution risk. The problem is the joint probability that all required innovations will succeed – this is represented by multiplying the probabilities of success, not by adding them together. For example, three independent projects, each with an attractive probability of success of 80 %, result in only a joint probability of success of just over 50 %, namely ($0.8 \times 0.8 \times 0.8 = 51.2\%$). While the individual decision-maker of the individual projects may be in a positive mood, a (virtual) central party faces a significantly different situation and decision.

Adoption chain risk is defined as the "extent to which partners must adopt your innovation before end users have a chance to evaluate the full value proposition" (Adner 2013, 34).

The critical point is to convince each partner on the way to the consumer – usually through an individual benefit calculation that is not limited to price, but also takes into account aspects of changing existing processes, tools and capabilities.

It seems that many elements of existing governance and strategy approaches can be used for individual organizations. At the same time, it becomes clear that additional dimensions strongly influence digital (innovation) ecosystems and need to be considered in the governance and strategy of the individual organization – not to mention common cross-organizational aspects in multilateral or even multi-leader ecosystems.

Lessons learned:
The Drakkensberg ecosystem faces significant adaptation chain and co-innovation risks. One approach that has worked well is to relax the (time) constraints and give each partner enough space to successfully adapt and innovate. This may be counter-intuitive in a "traditional world" often dominated by the idea

of first-mover advantage. But in an ecosystem, the validity of this concept is questionable. In fact, some issues are deliberately "parked" and covered by traditional processes in order not to be dependent on the speed, direction and success of legal adjustments at the cantonal and federal level, as in the case of fully digital and virtual notarizations. In addition, it was beneficial to decouple activities wherever possible and to carefully select the members of the "minimally viable ecosystem" – which includes lawyers and notaries of the entrepreneurs, but not the entrepreneur herself – in order to reduce the amount of supervision required. The concept of "minimal viable" also manifested itself in small and quick steps with reasonable effort and risk, much like the "affordable loss" approach used in the entrepreneurial world.

Execution risk is successfully mitigated by leveraging the excellence of each connected partner. Execution issues between partners are addressed quickly and effectively through short communication channels in regular video calls between all partners. However, more elaborate governance and coordination mechanisms are required as the ecosystem begins to grow.

6 Conclusions

The Drakkensberg ecosystem has been an exciting and rewarding journey for all partners. Over 60 registered companies and a record time of two hours for the entire startup process clearly mark great successes. There were many lessons to be learned and many more lie ahead on the path to hopefully a widely scaled ecosystem in the future. The most important aspects are:

The Drakkensberg ecosystem formed only because of its truly multilateral nature, with all partners acting at eye level. The joint value proposition of dramatically shortening the time to start a business played a key role. Coordination between partners has been very efficient and effective, but only with an implicit governance model.

Decoupling activities and relaxing (time) constraints proved to be key success criteria to mitigate pervasive ecosystem risks. Likewise, the use of elements from the entrepreneurial world such as "affordable loss" and small quick steps contributed to successful growth.

No single partner expects sufficient profit to justify investment across the ecosystem. Nevertheless, joint governance and strategy are becoming increasingly important to further expand the ecosystem. First steps have been taken by explicitly formulating guiding principles for the ecosystem and by deciding to develop a joint memorandum of understanding.

Overall, Drakkensberg is a good example of the dynamics and challenges of a small DLT ecosystem. In particular, scaling it is a time-consuming and complex task. Today, the exciting phase to significantly scale is right in front of the Drakkensberg ecosystem. While many challenges are on the horizon, the proven agility, motivation and trustworthiness of all partners over the past years are one – if not the – key success criteria for the road ahead.

Literature

Adner, R. (2013). The wide lens – What successful innovators see that others miss. Penguin Group, New York.

Adner, R. (2017). Ecosystem as structure: An actionable construct for strategy. Journal of Management. 43(1), 39-58, 2017.

Bogers, M. Sims, J., &. West, J. (2019). What is an ecosystem? Incorporating 25 years of ecosystem research. Academy of Management Proceedings. 2019, 1.

Gassmann, O., Frankenberger, K., & Csik, K. (2017). The business model navigator – 55 models that will revolutionise your business. Harlow Pearson Education Limited, London.

Hilb, M. (2016). New corporate governance – Successful board management tools. 5th ed. Springer, Berlin.

Hilb, M. (2018). Toward an integrated framework for governance of digitalization. In M. Hilb (ed.); Governance of digitalization – The role of boards of directors and top management teams in digital value creation, 2nd ed. Haupt, Bern.

Schimpel, U. (2019). blockchain project roadmap. IBM, May 19, https://www.ibm.com/blogs/think/uk-en/blockchain-project-roadmap